*The Truth Book s— enlightening the People!!!*

# EAT LIKE YOU GIVE A DAMN

**Volume One: Begin Your Lifestyle Transition!**

by Ray Stone

# *Eat Like You Give a Damn*
## *Volume One: Beginning Your Lifestyle Transition*
© 2009 **Ray Stone**
All Rights Reserved

\* Speaking Engagements
\* Life Coaching Packages
\* General Information

Contact Ra One Publications:
ra1publications@gmail.com
likeugivedamn@gmail.com
www.likeugiveadamn.com
(313) 397-5199

Cover Design & Layout: **Michael Angelo Chester**
All Photo Credits: **Rashid El (Ray Stone-El)**
Rear Cover Photo: **Samir Johnson**
**Copyright 2009**
**Ra One Publications**

*Coming Soon from Ra One Publications:*
**Products of Our Environment: Eat Like You Give a Damn Volume II**

No part of this book may be reproduced without formal, written permission.
Manufactured in the US Republic (Northwest Amexem)
10 9 8 7 6 5 4 3 2 1
For Library of Congress Data, See Publisher

# Message to the Reader

The information in this book is not intended to be prescriptive, in spite of the safety and simplicity of the things suggested for people suffering from chronic debilitating conditions. For the best results and additional guidance, the author suggests that all should be under the supervision of a doctor, chiropractor, osteopath, or a professional who is well studied in natural therapy, fasting, detoxification crises, and withdrawal symptoms under dietary changes.

This book makes no claim to offer a cure for aches and pains, colds, or chronic ailments like cancer, diabetes, arthritis, or heart diseases. Instead, it offers you a way of life that is in tuned with Nature's Laws to regenerate the body, heal it, regain its beauty and prolong its youth. Restore natural function.

The methods of healing that are suggested may not be in accord with the established consensus of the medical profession. This information is made available to all those who wish to investigate all known methods of healing. In time of sickness or accident, the individual will have to accept the responsibility of choosing ones doctor and your own method of treatment.

The gratifying experiences of thousands of brothers and sisters around the world have confirmed emphatically my belief in the authenticity and reliability of the principles delineated in this book.

The healing section of the book is written in layman's language. The technical papers cited should be consulted by doctors to evaluate the full potential of the ideas and data.

The author/publisher can assume no responsibility for the improper application or interpretation of the laws of nature contained in this book. No guarantee is implied and all actions pursued as a result of the material contained herein are at the sole risk of the reader. However, I feel that the benefits accruing from such procedures and practices far exceed the consequences of the use of medicine and poison for therapy. Right nutrition is the only path for providing diseased body with the material from which to rebuild itself with minimal discomfort.

The handbook itself is of low nutritional content and should never be eaten! Only digested.

✌ Peace, Love and Happiness to you all. I am humbly grateful to share this with you.

Search for the natural path and be in good health!!

This book and anything that I achieve in this life
is dedicated to my mother Lois Stone, who I love and admire with all my
heart. My mom allowed me to dream, and taught me to love and appreciate
life. Those are the greatest lessons I have ever received. I feel honored to have
been under your loving guidance.
(*I'm glad you chose me*).

As we have always said "I love you all the world Mom!" Thank you. Thank
you. Thank you. We make a great team!

Also to my ancestors: my dad Benjamin Stone
Uncle Art, Aunt Wanda, Aunt Barbara
We honor and miss you.

# Eat Like You Give a Damn
(The Handbook)
## The Ingredients:

| | |
|---|---|
| *Acknowledgments & Introduction* | iii-ix |
| Chapter 1: Clean Your Pipes | 1 |
| Chapter 2: Vacation | 9 |
| Chapter 3: The Protein Myth | 12 |
| Chapter 4: Eating Healthy is NOT too expensive | 19 |
| Chapter 5: Family Owned Farms | 24 |
| Chapter 6: Michigan Family Farm Information | 26 |
| Chapter 7: Reading is Fundamental | 30 |
| Chapter 8: Everyday Suicide (HFCS & Hydrogenated Oils) | 36 |
| Chapter 9: If you like 'this'…try 'this' | 42 |
| Chapter 10: The smooth way to a healthy lifestyle | 51 |
| Chapter 11: Where SHOULD you Grocery Shop | 53 |
| Chapter 12: STAY OUT OF THE DRIVE THRU!!! | 57 |
| Chapter 13: List of Local Restaurants | 58 |
| Chapter 14: Endangered Species | 63 |
| Chapter 15: Reverse Evolution: From the Farm to the Pharmacy | 67 |
| Chapter 16: Herb-ology | 71 |
| Chapter 17: Alternative Medicines | 75 |
| Chapter 18: Outro | 79 |
| Chapter 19: Food For Thought (The Love Movement) | 81 |
| Chapter 20: Glossary | 83 |

*Remember—Always Read the Ingredients!!!!*

# Acknowledgments

I want to express thanks to the many friends and family members that have helped me see this project to fruition. I am indebted to you all and truly appreciate you. Thank you for the support.

My sister **Pam**, whose kitchen is never safe when I am around, thanks for continuing to let me in! And listening. I love you, and the kids-there is nothing I won't do for you all. I still hit those cabinets when I come home.

Peace, love, and gratitude to: **Khadijah (Tu)**, **Jessica**, my cousins **Phyl** & **Alycia**, **Roxanne**, **CC**, **Sara**, **Nina**, **Berry**, **Samir**, my brother **Warren**—thank you all for letting me bounce ideas off of you. Life is nothing without people to share your feelings with.

To the many, many people I have connected with that helped start me on this path! I cannot thank you enough. My life has truly blossomed since this quest began.

Jess I've watched you argue with doctors and family about milk, candy, and medicine —trying to raise young **King** vegetarian is not easy in the *D*. I admire the effort, and it will all pay off. Never worry, he has everything he needs in you! You've inspired millions of people in this world and I am most definitely one of them. Thanks for your love and support.

King says it best, "No chicken! No hot dog!" He is more aware than some people already! That seed is firmly planted!

**Ylonda** & **Roxanne**, a lot of my book was written in tranquility of McGregor Bay (Bey), Canada. Thanks for inviting me to that paradise! And don't forget your boy next year! Peace Dave.

Rox you have listened to me preach, cussing out the world so many times over. I appreciate your support and belief in me. Great things will come to you too! (Watch the tea thing blow up!) 1120.

*Time is an illusion.*

**C Rose**, after reading notebook after notebook of my scribbling, you were the first person to ever tell me that I should consider writing for a living. I appreciate the foresight. Thank you, and my other BAM at 1631, for truly accepting me as family. I love you all.

**Tolliver**, you have more love inside you than anyone I have ever known. I miss you much! Laugh for me.

# Introduction

**Peace.**

I am so glad that you are reading this book! It is in your hands right now because there is a message in it for you; it has reached you for a reason.

This handbook was done from start to finish in love and good energy. There is only one goal and motivation behind it: improving people's health for good.

I've learned some amazing things in a short time that changed my life in many ways. I was thankful to be around (attract) people that "helped to" enlighten me. Through reading, listening, and blessing—I was able to evolve and grow. I was growing as fast as my locks (*partly because of my locks*). Things that I was made privy to have completely changed my life.

I want to share some of those things with you. I want to help you change your life as well.

What I really need you to understand is that I know that this is not easy. I know just how hard it is when you have been used to doing things the same way your entire life.

This is not an *arrogant* book. I don't look down upon anyone, nor do I feel I am better than any one of you either. We are the same—*I am you.*

I grew up eating 99-cent Big Macs, Whoppers, Lemonheads, Honey Buns, and drinking 2-liter Faygo's all day long. I know how you feel. I used to love me some cheese too!! I ordered EVERYTHING with extra cheese! I put ranch dressing on damn near everything back then. I have been there. I know it seems real hard to change things that you have been doing your entire life. I know exactly how that feels. I *know* it tastes good.

Since I have been vegan I hear the same type of things all the time: "Yo, that's good and all…but man, I don't know if I could eat like that".

What's so funny to me is that I used to say the ***same exact things*** to people who were vegan!! And I meant it! I can remember my whole family laughing at my niece Kenya when she first offered us all a delicious tofu scramble in the morning.

"O…naw, you can keep that 'stuff'…I'm gonna have 'real' food for breakfast," I maintained, frowning hard at her funny looking plate. That wasn't that long ago.

Trust me, I know exactly how it is when that stuff '*be*' looking weird to you!

So you see, I am you. We are each other.

Over the next few weeks, months, and years you can make major changes too! And you will be SO GLAD once you begin to evolve and understand.

This is the time in our world for CHANGE.

Use this handbook as a launch pad to begin that change. Begin to transition. Check out some of the suggested books and websites. Find some new restaurants and experience new foods. Explore buying food from farms & farmer's markets as opposed to huge supermarkets.

Even if you don't change everything overnight. That's ok. Start to take some steps right now. Be open to trying a new thing or two, go to the right venues, and it will snowball.

Clean your body inside. Moderate what you eat. Monitor it. READ THE LABELS of everything from now on.

Scrutinize EVERYTHING that you are going to allow inside your temple. What is it? Where did it come from? Who grew it? Who made it? What type of energy is behind it? That is where you want to go with it.

## *You are what you eat remember.*

Take some time to re-examine things that you eat and use on your body daily. That is YOUR temple! A temple should receive the utmost respect. Just like you respect your place of worship. You should respect your body more than anything!!

That is God's unique gift to you alone! Appreciate it and preserve it.

## *"They don't make 'em like they used to."*

That saying applies across the board: clothes, shoes, cars, furniture, houses, etc. The fast food, fast money society has affected everything. In haste to mass-produce everything today for as little as possible, they make cheap junk.

The food industry included. That is something that we definitely need to explore and re-evaluate. They feed that cheap junk to you and your family, flood the market with it, making it very convenient to get. It is up to you to keep it out of your body.

We have to become more conscious about things that we are putting inside. What is more important than that?

Your body is such a precious gift; you can't just put anything inside it! Think about how well you have to know someone before you even consider letting them into your home or into your personal space. Make at least some effort to know this food a little better before you eat it and it becomes part of you.

## *Temet Nosce*

So much focus today is put on weight loss and physical appearance in general. We have to come to the understanding that things work from the inside out. Control what you put INSIDE your body—and you CAN control your physical appearance quite easily.

It's really *that* simple.

You'll notice that I hardly talk about specific exercises or regular working out at all in this handbook. Movement is a huge key to health of course, but trust me, when you clean out your insides and feel that child like energy restored. You will move! I guarantee it!

You will run the stairs faster without even noticing. You will walk more because you feel better, and lighter. Your skin will glow people will compliment you and ask what you are doing. Your sex life will be better!

Better health is the fountain of youth—your energy level will dictate you becoming more active in general.

Do not think of it as changing your diet. Change your lifestyle and philosophy towards the way you treat your body. Our current approach to life is short sighted and backwards.

Volume 1 of this series is the beginning of your transition. It is designed to give readers some practical ways to bring about changes in life RIGHT NOW. This is indeed the time for change in this country. The current president is a good symbol of that, especially within the urban community.

Lets cleanse out the ugly past and move forward light, healthy, and free. We can change the world, reclaim our empire and rightful place in our homeland—it starts with our own temples.

I know its rough when you are used to the food you have been eating. Its familiar and it tastes good. Once you initiate change, things will snowball for you. You will enjoy the progress and learning new things makes life really exciting.

## *Revolutionary Health*

My books are very straightforward, hardcore projects. Forgive the tone of the words and any harsh language. I understand that this is a very sensitive subject for people. Health issues are hard to deal with in every way. But I am merely bringing some simple, yet important facts to your attention. This is real talk.

The way disease and health issues are affecting our community is very alarming. It commands our immediate attention. We are basically eating ourselves to death.

It's hard for me to hide my passion about it. I have to repress my feelings at every family cookout and/or gathering—and just about everywhere else. At times it feels like the bottom line is people could care less about it. (Nobody gives a damn.)

So forgive me if at any juncture this text sounds like I am talking 'at' you. That is only hints of subdued passion perhaps leaking out. My subjective writing style may not meet the standards that you might be used to.

Please don't let that distract you from the information that is put together for you here. A lot of work went into this handbook. It is very valuable. There is definitely a message inside for you. This work comes purely from my heart.

This is but my first official publication. I am a work in progress myself. You have my commitment; I will continue seeking growth as an author and communicator.

So let's grow together.

You think about exploring some of the ideas in this handbook. Buckle your seat belt for the forthcoming books. They are very powerful! Decide this is the time for you to initiate some healthy changes in your life. You will be so glad that you did!

## Projects on deck:

Volume two of this series will be available October 2009: **PRODUCTS OF OUR ENVIRONMENT** (*Eat Like you Give a Damn volume 2*). Ouch! Volume II features an in depth look at some of the products that we use in our homes, and on our bodies. Exploring just how much impact they can have on our health and the environment. Volume 2 will also dig deeper into the dangers of the food industry. It is a must have as you continue your personal evolution! Stay tuned.

**THE ARTIFICIAL WORLD** (*Eat Like you Give a Damn volume 3*) is scheduled for release in the spring of 2010. It is a powerhouse! It focuses more on the philosophy and energy aspects of life. It covers way more than just food. It is about enhancing and rediscovering humanity in the fast paced world in which we dwell. It is the most thought provoking book in the series. It is a true (third) eye opener!

The interactive website www.likeugiveadamn.com is currently under construction and should be fully tested, up and running by July 2009. It will include reviews, video recipes, meal plan suggestion, links to local producers, parenting advice in regards to food, natural remedies, FAQ's, and much more. It will grow as we do and fully support your lifestyle transition. Stay connected with people going through the same thing you are!

This summer the **1st Annual "GREEN" Vegan Cookout** is going to rock Belle Isle!! Check the website and my Facebook for details. It will be an educational afternoon with strictly vegan foods, local beers, and beautiful people. Hope to see you there!

The aim is to eventually establish large support groups where ideas and energy can be bounced off of one another. We are in this journey together.

For book orders, any inquiries, comments or concerns, and/or to get on the e-mail list —send all emails to: likeugiveadamn@gmail.com

I am eager to work with any and all groups interested in getting together and creating change in their communities. Any positive ideas you have bring them to the table and lets try to put them in motion.

The ultimate goal is to connect people with people. We have to learn to stop supporting huge corporations and begin to get all our products and services from other people. Barter. That has to become the way of life going forward.

It all starts here.

Your first area of focus should be on cleaning and rebuilding your temple in 2009 and changes will surely happen inside and around you! Peace and blessings!

*Let's get to it.*

# Chapter 1
# *Clean Your Pipes*

### *Why Colon Cleanse?*
Cleaning the colon is an excellent (nearly mandatory) first step toward changing your entire life and health for good! Get rid of the waste material trapped inside and rediscover youth and natural energy. It will leave you feeling like a brand new person!

On a daily basis we shower to clean our bodies. We make sure our clothes are clean and maintained. At some point we need to make an effort to clean the inside of our bodies and digestive system.

**Why? The average American person is carrying between 7 and 25 pounds of waste material *INSIDE* their body!!!** If you have been eating the average American diet, or anything close to it, you *definitely* need to consider flushing out your body in order to restore its natural function.

The entire length of the human digestive system is 30 feet long. That is 30 feet of little, narrow, twisting pipes—from the small intestines, through the large intestine (colon) and out the bottom. The diameter of that piping is very small. Any clogging in that pipeline eventually puts a strain on the body in some way. That is the absolute ROOT of all health problems.

Things we ingest like meat, alcohol, flour, and sugar are extremely difficult for the body to process, that confusion eventually leads to a build up of fecal matter in your system. Any white substance, like sugar, flour, white rice, etc.—has been heavily processed and stripped of all natural food value. Your body does not even recognize it and cannot digest it.

Meats, for instance, even chicken and fish can take 1 to 2 whole days to work its way out of the entire human digestive track. But we'll often eat chicken or fish, (let alone beef or pork) 2 or 3 times in a single day! EVERY SINGLE DAY!

**Where is all of it going?** There is only one exit. How many times a day are you sitting on the toilet? If it is not as many times as you are eating, or, if you are eating right before bed—then where could all that excess waste be going? Nowhere. You are carrying it around inside!

***You need to flush those pipes!*** Waste builds up inside your body just like it would anywhere else!

Imagine how your closet would look after years and years without you cleaning it; over the years things accumulate everywhere. If you want to get some new things, cleaning it is a mandatory first step. Getting rid of the old junk allows room for your new fly things.

Your internal "piping"—after days, months, and years of eating becomes cluttered with matter. You have to flush those pipes in order to keep yourself healthy and flowing correctly. Strain and imbalance inside the body is what sets the table for dis-ease.

Before taking a chemical *medicine* for any type of *symptom*—consider cleansing or fasting. Allow your body a chance to heal on its own. When flowing correctly, your body can balance itself. **Let nature flush out the root of the ailment—without the drugs or knives. That is how a free flowing system is designed to work. Give it a chance!**

Cleansing the body is somewhat like an oil change is for you vehicle. Having oil gunk, and dirty oil will ultimately shorten the life of a car. **Removing the old sludge and adding fresh oil allows the car to run smoothly. The same things can be said of the excess gunk inside the body.** Clean your digestive engine every 300 meals from now on. You are probably overdue, and the symptoms you experience serve as the warning light.

There are nerve endings inside the colon that correspond to every area of the body, therefore, the symptoms of dis-ease might surface anywhere in the body. The root of ALL health issues lies in the colon: aches & pains, sluggishness, grouchiness, tendonitis, eye problems, kidney stones, yeast infections, etc. You name it.

Waste material lining the colon hardens inside of the warm body. Lined with that hard layer of waste, colon walls become rigid and are no longer "spongy". Thus preventing the body from ridding itself of harmful, toxic materials through the exit. Your blood is then forced to keep harmful things inside, instead of releasing them through the colon like it would do in a free flowing system. That IS the onset of dis-ease and imbalance in the body.

Blockages have a dual negative effect. Excess waste also prevents the body from properly absorbing minerals from your food.

Once you have decided to change your eating habits, it only makes sense that you start by cleansing yourself out and flushing those pipes. That is a huge step towards a healthy existence! Take it!

## *How do you clean your pipes?*

☙Always remember to drink plenty of fresh water! It is absolutely essential.

That is one thing that you can do ***right now*** to improve your overall health.

Drink lots of water and tea. Cut out the bottled juices. Cut down the beer & wine. When you do have a beer or a glass of wine—be sure to have several glasses of water along with it.

When you drink enough water it naturally suppresses your appetite and gives your body a chance to regulate your weight. Water flushes the system out. It is one of the most important things to do for maintaining health. Your body is composed of over 70% water—having sufficient amounts of water everyday helps to keep everything flowing properly.

Insufficient water in your system creates ideal conditions for blockages & build up. Keep your system flowing, especially if you are cleansing in any way! A cleanse cannot be effective without ample water to flush out the waste trapped inside.

Raw fruits and vegetables are composed mainly of water just like your body. A juicy apple or watermelon is nature's purist water supply! Eating lots of raw fruits and veggies will help maintain balance and flow. ☯

## *Colon Hydrotherapy (A Colonic)*

A Colonic is a process where warm mineral water is shot gently up the anus into the colon & large intestine. This process softens and dislodges the hard waste matter lining the walls of the colon. That is the waste you need to remove. Over the years it has become impacted on your colon walls.

**And no, it is certainly not the most *pleasant* procedure in the world.** But you have to be very mature about it and understand it as something that can be vital for your overall health.

You should consider it; at least GOOGLE it and find out more about the process and its benefits. Although it is a bit uncomfortable—true enough—so is colon cancer, diabetes, arthritis, allergies, yeast infections, and the rest of the long list of ailments that can be attributed to blockages inside the colon.

Many natural health practitioners recommend that you do a colonic, or a series of colonics, during the change of seasons when nature is shifting.

## *Colon Cleaning System*

There are many different colon-cleaning products that you can utilize to help rid yourself of excess junk. I have personally used *Colonix* (www.drnatura.com), a 3-part system consisting of: fiber powder, anti-parasite pills, and a detoxification tea. I found it to be VERY effective.

Ms. Rashid, in the Eastern market and the Russell Street Bazaar, has a (*Black Seed*) product that is nearly identical. It is cheaper and you don't have to order it online. I have not tried that product as of yet, but it is constructed quite the same.

The systems are generally easy to take, but it will require consistency and dedication. They recommend at least 60-90 days your first time cleansing. You have to remember that this is many YEARS of waste that you are trying to remove from your body. YOU WANT THAT STUFF OUT!!

It seems like a long time, but it is not. It's not difficult to take the cleanser at all. It is 3 parts: Anti-parasite pills in the morning with a glass of water. 15 minutes after that, you drink this herbal fiber powder in a breakfast smoothie. I STRONGLY recommend that you make a smoothie, add the powder, and add a multi-vitamin of some sort. Sweeten it with Maple syrup or Agave nectar. (I will demonstrate this in the seminar).

The last step is to steep and drink the cleansing tea (which tastes really good) right before bed.

It is not harsh at all. You can leave the house without any worry about running to the bathroom. It's nothing like that. Your body will adjust to your consistent pattern—and in the morning you will go, and A LOT comes out!

With each elimination it feels like you lose extra weight and gain extra energy. You can really feel a major difference a week or two into it. You will bounce off of the toilet.

A healthy smoothie, as opposed to doughnuts, coffee, or cereal, is an excellent way to start your day. That is a really good habit to get into. Have your fruit ready to go in the morning and it will take only minutes. You can fit it into even the busiest schedules. The first two steps are first thing in the morning, and the last one is right before bed.

*It is very workable.*

However, if you feel the kit is too much, there are a number of detoxification teas and products that you can choose from. Many of them, like the Dr. Schulze (drschulze.com) cleaning system are designed to clean all of your internal organs. Research some of the many cleansing products out there. (Natural Food Patch has a big selection of them.)

Whatever you decide, spend some time and energy towards cleansing your insides. You will notice that your body functions better after removing waste.

You feel more 'responsiveness' inside your temple, similar to how a vehicle performs better after a tune-up. It feels amazing! I experienced absolutely incredible results with the cleansing system:

- My hair and nails started growing noticeably faster
- I instantly stopped taking Clariton and Benadryl as my harsh allergy symptoms suddenly disappeared. (NO DAIRY PRODUCTS!)
- I saw all kinds of stool come out of me—shapes, sizes, colors and lengths!! It may be nasty, but its way nastier that it was INSIDE MY BODY!
- My body odor was totally different. I would never, ever get "funky". Even if I forgot to put on deodorant. (I started forgetting all the time.)
- My stomach started getting flatter, without me doing any sit-ups!

Overall, I just noticed that my body was completely functioning better! I had lots of energy. I wouldn't get sleepy at all after I ate. (Even at the firehouse, where naptime is ritual!) I would sleep hard and sound during the night and have those really good long dreams. (Everyone I know that did a cleanse said the exact same thing about their dreams.) I woke up fully recharged.

I developed a zest for life that has never left. Excited for each new day. Its a natural buzz, I'm trying to pass it to y'all! I want you to experience that!

Do something to cleanse your body. You will feel and look years younger and not look back!

## *Fasting*

Speaking of putting energy into it, fasting is the natural way to clean. It gives your body a chance to cleanse and balance on its own. No purchase necessary; just your own discipline and dedication to your body.

The *longer* you fast, the *better*. The body can heal itself of anything given the time. After 24 hours without being given food to deal with, your body goes into a cleansing mode. Your internal resources focus their energy on correcting any issues inside your system. Fasting equates to the best medicine and best doctor there is at your service… nature!

The problem is most of us have been eating badly for a long, long time. That is why I recommend a colonic (or a few), or a colon cleaning system initially. However, fasting regularly will definitely keep your body in proper balance.

It takes a high level of discipline to fast for any length of time. The longer you can fast, 3, 7, 14 days or longer—the better it is for clearing your system. It gives your digestive system a much-needed break.

Don't think of it in terms of just starving yourself. Look at it as allowing divine nature to perform surgery on your body. Spend time still and at rest during your fast as much as possible. It will clear your head as well. Let your spirit recharge. Anticipate the new levels of health and energy that await after your chemical free surgery!

**The Master Cleanse** is a popular fast where you drink "lemonade", (consisting of Water, Lemon juice, Maple syrup, & cayenne pepper) to quench your hunger and clean your insides. People stay on that for 3, 7, 14 days or longer. That is something you might want to do at the change of season.

You can fast doing only fruit and water, as fruit is a natural cleanser; or only water and teas. You can utilize any type of fast you want actually.

Bringing your mind into the fold during a fast is very important. Learn how to ascend past low-level cravings. Be smarter than your stomach, and you will reach higher spiritual levels as well. Learn to master your temple.

Whatever method you choose for yourself personally—make sure you put some focus and energy on cleaning the inside of your temple (body).

Do it on some type of schedule. Just like you change your oil on the car every 3,000 miles or every 3 months. The most logical time to cleanse is at the change of season, as the nature around you is changing. Clean yourself and get off to a light, fresh start each season!

Check out some books on fasting and cleansing. Get your google on about the colon and the problems that dirty insides can produce.

*Decide right now to make better health choices for your temple.*

## Dirty Thoughts

Cleansing your insides has a dual positive effect. Along with improved physical function, it can also clear clutter within the mind. This allows you to think more freely, opening you to fresh new thoughts and ideas.

That is why people's dreams are so intense during (and after) a cleanse. Your mental load lightens. When your insides are physically cluttered and blocked, your mentality is cluttered and blocked as well.

Cleansing the insides helps to release all the old garbage energy that is stored inside your body everywhere: the colon, the muscles, the joints and even the mind.

You know how mentally refreshing it feels when you get the entire house completely clean, the kids are gone for the whole weekend—and you can have some wine and just relax? Well, when you cleanse your body, it eases your mind that same way!

So after that harsh divorce, hard break up, or losing a job—go get a colonic! Or fast for a week or so. Release that old stale energy from your being and clear the way new experiences. Don't stuff yourself with ice cream and cookies for comfort. That helps clog and block everthing more.

Don't carry all that energy and emotion inside. Let it flow out and move on like the vessel of water that we are.

Dirt and clutter cause confusion and uneasiness. The early signs of disharmony *inside* the body are people that we all know. Things like: a negative attitude, depression, envy, impatience, fear, mistrust, over thinking, suspicion, worry, etc. Those are all early indications of discord inside the body.

That is part of the reason that people end up in the same type of life situations. We attract the same experiences over and over again in part because we never purge the waste. Learn to treat life situations (lessons) like your body does food: digest it, take what you can utilize from experiences, (learn from them) and totally eliminate the rest.

**Free yourself!!!**
So many people I know are flat out UNWILLING to try anything new. They look at my food, frown, and say it "looks" nasty—like 12 year olds. **How is it that every party I have been to since I was born, I just know it is going to be some damn chicken wings and spaghetti?!** Same. Old. A lot of the reason people are holding on to the same old s*%$, is because they are literally holding on to the same old s*%$.

Of course it is going to seem very hard to think about giving up chicken—especially when inside you are literally stuffed with old chicken! That WILL make you crave it! It becomes a part of your insides. Cleaning yourself out allows the NATURAL, innate cravings to be recognized.

Having an open and free mind is vitally important as you begin to learn healthier ways of eating and living. Some of this stuff may be totally foreign to you. This handbook contains only the start of some major changes in your life.

You are going to be introduced to new foods and cuisines that you may have never seen or heard of before. You can't experience new things and grow with a closed mind.

As you learn more and clear your mind—your perspective will change. Your palette will change. You will see what really does look nasty. Your eyes will literally be cleaner. The smells won't be as appealing to you. There are many wonderful natural things for you to learn about and experience. First we have to get off of the processed chemical "foods".

Given a chance, your body will always heal itself. You will crave exactly what you need to balance yourself in a healthy system. The processed stuff prevents nature from taking its course. You end up craving fast food and crap, because it is trapped inside your system. That's why it is on your mind all the time. (Not to mention it is on the television and on billboards everywhere, constantly in your sight. They literally try to stuff us with food in this country, to keep us full, sick, and dumb. WAKE UP!)

*Cleansing can help rid you of old habits as well. You will become more open to experience new things and you will want to grow as a natural being. Let it the old stuff go! Live freely, clearly, and recognize the infinite possibilities that lie within your nature.*

## Chapter 2

# *Vacation*

*We go on vacation to relax and get away. It is peaceful and quiet. We get to break our daily routine, giving up the usual rips & runs, opting for the other r & r—rest and relaxation.*

We need that break in our lives! It feels good just to break the routine of life and have some down time for yourself.

The "workers union" on the inside of our bodies that would have the biggest complaints would be the digestive system and the elimination departments! They never get a break—unless a mean supervisor like the flu shuts the whole 'plant' completely down.

The point is we eat EVERY SINGLE DAY…without fail! Sometimes after the club, scarf down those late night, 'I'm just drunk as hell' meals. Or just because something tastes good, we'll often eat way past being full. Eating has become a daily pleasure for us these days.

Everyone says to me as we talk about health at some point that they just "LOVE TO EAT!!!"

Most people could probably survive on only half of the food (and protein) that we actually consume. America is the fattest, most greedy country in the world.

The danger is that so many of these new ingredients are totally foreign to the body. We stuff ourselves with processed ingredients that our bodies don't even recognize.

Making matters worse, we don't drink nearly enough water. That would help the body flush some of the junk out! But who really drinks 8 glasses of water a day? Alcohol and sugar, both dehydrate you. When you factor that in—we are not drinking NEARLY enough water in general.

So the poor digestive system and elimination departments are overworked as it is, plus confused, AND working in the worst possible conditions. On top of that they get NO days off, very few breaks, and NO vacation!! How would you respond if your job was like that?!

They are bound to get behind, leaving undigested residue inside the body! Eventually, they will quit on us! Can you blame them?

THEY NEVER GET A DAY OFF! When is the last 24-hours that you have fasted and completely given your body a rest?

When have you said, "you know what belly, you are getting bigger, and I am just going to give you the whole week, or at least a few days off." When have you said that? You are the CEO of your body! Consider giving the temple a break from time to time.

It doesn't have to be NO food at all, although it certainly can. And if you are dealing with a major illness, that is one of the best cures. Let the digestive system shut down for a while and send its resources to the 'healing' office.

Again, nature knows how to balance itself, without laboratory chemicals and drugs!

Nature has been here for ages; a lot of these new chemicals are man made laboratory creations, they are not natural. Stick with things that are of nature, which is tried and true. Try to always keep that in mind.

Why not give your digestive system the easy assignments sometimes?

Eat live foods (raw fruits & vegetables) 1 or 2 days out of the week. That is an excellent habit to adopt after you have cleansed yourself. Ensure you won't fill yourself back up with garbage, although your eating habits will naturally change. Keep your body clean with your diet and you will have loads of energy and be healthy for a long time.

Where can you begin? From this day forward, challenge yourself. Don't eat meat on the weekends. If you are a meat eater, at least give your system that little break.

Eventually maybe ONLY eat meat on the weekends. Give yourself small, tangible challenges like that. Go to farmer's markets and learn some new foods!

Live like that and you will experience life like never before. Enjoy a new level of health. By constantly learning new things, you will stay young forever!

Don't be a mean boss. Give your body a break!!

*Remember the inside of your body needs a well-deserved break from time to time too!*

# Chapter 3
# The Protein Myth

I get asked the question nearly every single day! Literally. As soon as people find out I'm vegan, its "well where do you get your protein?"

There is a HUGE protein myth in America. (Dare I say, conspiracy?) People are firmly convinced that you need lots and lots of protein, and that meat is the best source of that protein.

*That is simply not the case.*

The meat industry pushes hard to sell their mass produced, diseased animals. (You know they do not have to label cloned meat at all.) They put millions of dollars into advertisement in all forms of media.

My favorite is the commercial with old Granny jumping rope in 'church clothes', as the smooth voice asks, "have you had your 'Tyson protein' today?"

It's totally ridiculous. (If Granny is eating that Tyson everyday, she is probably on some type of pill too! Sugar, Pressure, something!)

While your body does need its sufficient amounts of protein, it is not THE vital thing for your development by any means. You shouldn't be looking at it like that. You need vitamins, minerals, iron, etc. But they just don't get the enormous amount of publicity that protein does.

Chicken breast, egg whites, salmon, or whatever you are eating for your 'daily protein' is by far not the only source of protein. It is NOT the best source of protein either. You should develop a wide variety of protein sources.

There are as many as 20 different strands of Amino Acids that your body uses to make a complete protein. A diverse diet of different fruits, vegetables, grains, legumes (beans), is the best way to get all of the diverse building blocks for protein.

Eating a lot of cooked protein is not a very good idea at all, because your body must break that protein into amino acids before it can use it anyway. That makes it a 2-step process, adding stress to your system, which can age the body prematurely.

If we use meat as a primary source of protein, cooking destroys at least one of the essential amino acids needed for building enzymes and healthy tissue. Cooking can destroy 40 to 85 percent of the protein available in most food.

Believe it or not, we can actually get ALL the protein you need from raw plants and fruit! YES—even fruit has protein!! You won't ever see that on a commercial though!

Just think about it logically: cows grow hundreds of pounds of protein flesh on a natural diet of simple grass, which hardly contains ANY protein at all! How can that be? The cow doesn't have to eat a lot of protein!

Yet they've convinced us that we need to eat some high protein diet to get our natural protein supply?! That doesn't make any sense at all!

Our bodies will develop *pure muscle naturally*, if we eat within our nature as well.

The list of raw food, vegan animals are among the strongest beings on earth. The Gorilla, for instance, only eats fruits, herbs, and nuts—yet can bench press 4000 pounds! No protein shakes necessary! The Elephant, the Horse, the Bull, the Rhinoceros, the Giraffe—nobody questions where they're getting their protein from! They are all strict raw food vegetarians.

They obviously don't have commercials and media outlets in the forest. KILL YOUR TV!!!

The over consumption of animal protein really overloads the body, eventually creating large amounts of excess mucus in our system like dairy products. The mucus lines your internal organs, compromising both the respiratory and digestive systems. Asthma, allergies and other health issues can eventually ensue.

Excess protein has also been linked with osteoporosis, kidney disease, calcium stones in the urinary tract, and some cancers.

Why is it advertised and promoted it like it is daily? Because it is big business, they are selling products! 1 out of every 3 American commercials is about food. Most of it is for mass-produced synthetic mess.

We should not be eating disgusting dead animals period. Much less feeding it to our children. That does not belong in our Temple at all. That is why it ends up rotting, decaying, and fermenting inside the intestines and colon.

Milk doesn't do the body good! But they pay actors to put that disgustingly foul film moustache on their lips to keep us buying milk. Selling us another product. Reinforcing another myth. Dairy products are not really good for you.

Even if you are still thinking that dairy IS good for you and/or that lean protein is needed as part of a healthy diet; please keep in mind that these are just NOT the same animals and/or animal products as they were just 15 or 20 years ago.

The animals we are eating today are sick themselves. It is not the same animals that our grandparents who lived to be 95 grew up on! They have NEW feeds, NEW chemicals, NEW steroids, etc. that are in the fold today.

The media machine is more powerful than ever too—keeping people thinking one way.

***Keep that TV off and you won't be so hungry!!!***

No myth is greater than the protein one! I have been in thousands of debates about it.

But here is the bottom line, while we spend SO much time talking about protein: have you EVER, at any time in your life, even once known anyone suffering from a protein deficiency? Or heard about anyone hospitalized for that?

> *Don't worry I'll wait...*
> —Katt Williams

Certainly you know no one that has died from protein deficiency right? Of course not!! It's unheard of. Not getting enough protein should be the least of your worries! Americans are more at risk of eating too much protein than too little.

But millions suffer from and die of Heart Attacks, Strokes, Diabetes, High Blood Pressure, Cancer Treatment, and the like everyday. The strain put on the body trying to digest, breakdown, and eliminate cooked animal 'protein' is a major reason why. And that is a **FACT**!

That won't be on the commercials either. Just do a Google search about the widely recognized complications of consuming too much protein.

Over stressing the body in any way causes imbalance and disorder, creating the conditions for dis-ease. The majority of our bodies inner resources are used in the digesting of so much food. Leaving our immune system weaker, stressing, and aging the body.

That would not be an issue at all if we just ate fruits, vegetables, grains, beans, and nuts—more natural protein sources.

If you are vegetarian/vegan, or thinking about making the switch for a healthier life and people are constantly asking and harassing you (because they will), "where are you getting your protein from?"

Hold up a piece of fresh, locally grown fruit and tell them proudly... "*Everywhere*!"

*You see all this food that grows from the earth, why do want to eat dead animals? Go Vegetarian!!"*

## *Animal Protein with Vegetable Protein Equivalents*

Eggs. . . . . . . . . . . . . . . . . . . . . . . . . . . . . . . . . . . . . . . . *Navy Beans & Black Beans*
Fish. . . . . . . . . . . . . . . . . . . . . . . . . . . . . . . . . . . . . . . . . . . . . . . *Millet, Lentils*
Beef. . . . . . . . . . . . . . . . . . . . . . . . . . . . . . . . . . . . . . . . . . . . . *Wheat, Barley*
Cheese. . . . . . . . . . . . . . . . . . . . . . . . . *Soybeans, Corn (Rice Cheese, Soy Cheese)*
Poultry. . . . . . . . *Garbanzo Beans, Raw Peanuts, Sunflower Seeds, Green Peas*

## *Other High Protein Food Sources*

| Soybeans | Chick Peas | Kidney Beans |
| Adzuki Beans | Other Beans | Tofu |
| Lentils | Almonds | Other Nuts and Seeds |
| Kamut | Quinoa | Other Whole Grains |
| Spelt | Tempeh | TVP |
| Banana | Avocado | Cucumber |

## *Good, Complete Protein Combinations*

- *Beans and Brown Rice*
- *Corn and Green Beans*
- *Corn and Lima Beans*
- *Millet and Green Beans*
- *Garbanzo Beans and Seeds*
- *Tofu and Rice (Brown, Wild, Basamati, etc.)*
- *Whole Grain Pasta (Wheat, Brown Rice, etc.), Sesame Seeds and Corn*
- *Bulger Wheat and Dried Beans*
- *Quinoa with Banana (good breakfast combo!)*

People associate MILK with CALCIUM (the commercials have us thinking that way). You may get asked a lot when you go non-dairy, where are you (or your children) getting your calcium from? Medical doctors will not recommend giving up dairy for the calcium it provides. The Medical Association has educated (*brainwashed*) them into thinking that way.

We have to do our own homework. Green leafy vegetables, such as kale or collard greens, are actually much better than milk as a calcium source! Without all of the mucus and fat milk brings into the table.

Milk is very low in iron. Drinking milk can also cause blood loss from the intestinal tract, depleting the body's iron supply. Human beings are among the only animals that will drink the milk of another species. It's disgusting really.

Drinking a cow's milk? How did that become normal? Raise your hand if you would EVER put your mouth on a cow's nipple and drink from it! Really…it's not natural.

Humans are also the only animals that drinks milk period after the infant stage of life! Over 80% of people are lactose intolerant. Does that tell you anything about it being unnatural?

You should really consider getting totally OFF of dairy products! I know you love cheese—and "fake" cheeses are NO replacement. I used to love it too! Love your health even more! I really love not having sinus problems and harsh hay fever now that I've totally cut dairy.

The human body starts to slowly lose calcium after you've reached the age 30 or so, losing too much leads to fragile bones and/or osteoporosis. A lot of our elders seem to break their hip bones in even minor falls, as the bone has become quite fragile over the years.

Diets that are high in animal protein are more likely to cause more calcium loss than a plant based diet. Eating, digesting, and passing animal products takes its toll on your entire body. Vegetarians in general, tend to have stronger bones than meat eaters.

High sodium (Lawry's), caffeine, or smoking are also factors that lead to a higher than normal rate of calcium loss.

Exercise is good for keeping strong bones. Exposure to sun allows the body to make its own vitamin D. Calcium from fruits and vegetables, along with activity and sun, is the best formula to keep calcium in the bones.

# HIGH CALCIUM FOODS

## *VEGETABLES (MG per 1 cup)*

| | | |
|---|---|---|
| Broccoli (62) | Brussell Sprouts (56) | Butternut Squash (84) |
| Carrots (40) | Cauliflower (20) | Collards (266) |
| Kale (94) | Sweet Potato (76) | |

## *Other Calcium Sources*

| | | |
|---|---|---|
| Black Turtle Beans | Navy Beans | Soy Milk (fortified) |
| Northern Beans | Soy Beans | Tofu |
| White Beans | OJ (fortified) | |

## *Iron Woman*

Pregnant women quite often suffer from an iron deficiency. It is far more common in women than in men. Ladies you should be mindful of it. It is often not diagnosed, but you can very well be suffering the symptoms.

When you find yourself running around with kids, eating a fast paced diet, it can lead to low levels of iron. If you are tired or lethargic, thinking you need to get more rest, or need a "mommy" break—you could very well be running low on iron.

Here is a list of some high-iron foods that you can incorporate regularly into your diet to ensure that you have the energy you need to raise a healthy future.

## *High Iron Foods*

| | | |
|---|---|---|
| Dried Fruits | Molasses | Chick Peas |
| Black-eyed Peas | Pinto beans | Whole Grains |
| Dried figs | Sesame seeds | Other seeds |
| Prune Juice | Leafy Green Veggies | Artichoke |

## Chapter 4
# *Eating Healthy is not too expensive*

Don't believe the hype! This does not have to be the case. This ugly rumor is just yet another distraction that will prevent you from attempting to make necessary changes in your life. The only thing you can't afford is to buy into that.

It is all about knowing where to shop and eating as much local, fresh food as possible. Michigan has a lot of family owned farms where produce is fresh and very affordable. You will find that it is much cheaper and fresher than a commercial grocery store.

Community based farms are also becoming more popular, There could be one in your area. Check with the Grown in Detroit organization (detroitagriculture.org). Open yourself to the idea of supporting produce that is grown right in your area. There is even a Garden Resource program that assists those seeking to grow food in the city.

This spring consider growing something yourself! Start a small garden this year. Even if you start very small, with a couple of herb or pepper plants—get into the mindset of producing food, as opposed to always being a consumer. That is an invaluable lesson for young people.

Seeds are dirt-cheap (no pun intended). Plant and water them and you are on your way. Imagine tasting tomato sauce with your own home grown tomatoes and basil. That's as fresh as you can possibly get! Compare that to a chemically preserved jar of the leading brand!! There is no comparing the taste or the nutritional value. Eat as much fresh food as possible.

### *Farmer's Markets*

If you are not going to grow food, buy it directly from the people that do. Get your produce from a Farmer's Market. Eastern Market is open year round, housing a large number of local farmers. Several communities around the area have farmer's markets throughout the week as well.

Eating fresh produce sold to you by the very person who grew and picked it is about as close to a natural process as you can get. Otherwise try fruit & vegetable markets like Randazzo's (which is really affordable) or Westborn (which is a bit overpriced). These venues have fresh produce as well.

Sometimes, honestly, any extra money is worth it when talking about things your are going to eat. You are going to put that INSIDE your body (temple)! You should want nothing but the finest, most natural ingredients.

We definitely try not to put cheap clothes and things ON our bodies. You don't get all your shoes at Payless do you? You find a way to pay for better shoes. So you damn sure shouldn't cut corners when it comes to something we are going to put INSIDE our bodies!

Think about it like that sometimes.

I see people around the *D* with head to toe matching outfits all the time. Taking the time to make sure every little thing "coordinates". What's sad is that they are still eating processed, synthetic, 99-cent bullshit food—which is NO MATCH for the wonderful, divine machine that is the human body! In doing that, we neglect the thing that matters most. Mocking our Creator.

So far, shopping for produce from a local farmer's market is cheaper while offering better quality than a commercial grocer. At this point you could be eating healthier and spending less.

## *Meat the Parents*

If you are still eating meat, I would encourage you to look into a local farm (several are listed for you later in this handbook). Where meat is produced the old fashioned way, not shot with all types of drugs, and cloned or whatever else. ***KNOW WHERE YOUR FOOD IS COMING FROM.***

Purchasing meat from local farms is a very realistic option. Do not rush to think it is inconvenient because it may be a new concept to you. The information is listed right here for you, and it is worth looking into.

It may cost slightly more, but you know when it really pays off? When the news reports that next "danger" or "meat recall", your family won't have to worry about that. Keep your family healthy and safe.

Seek better food quality than that offered at large chain grocery stores with brand named packages. You do not want food that comes from that sort of big corporate business. Get the freshest, most natural meat possible. Period.

Those small neighborhood grocers have disgusting meat. They dye it to keep it colored. Its old, and rotting. That meat has been dead for who knows how long?!

Taking the time to get food that will keep you healthy saves you money in other ways as well. You won't need to keep running to doctors or pharmacies for a bunch of medicines. Your health and well-being is absolutely priceless!

I strongly recommend you explore dealing directly with family farms. It is the only meat you should even consider eating these days! (Go vegan!)

Food Travels on average 1500—2500 miles! When we buy local food it is fresher, it helps to save the environment, and preserves natural resources. We should be choosing 'naturally' grown Michigan produce over 'organic' produce from way across the globe all day. Especially when you can deal directly with the farmer.

*Birdtown Community Garden on Cass north of King. In Cass Corridor! Community gardening in the city is becoming popular. Vacant lots can turn into opportunities to produce food. That is the way we need to think going forward!*

## *Metro Detroit Area Farmers Markets*

**Northwest Detroit Farmers' Market (every Thurday)**
15000 Southfield Fwy, in the parking lot of the Bushnell Congregational Church, Detroit; open 4-8 p.m. every Thursday, June through September.
Hosts nearly 20 vendors that carry a variety of locally grown produce, baked goods, meats, eggs, cheeses and teas. Urban grown produce can be bought here, as well as organic pies and honey.

**Wayne State Wednesday Farmers' Market**
5201 Cass Ave., in front of Prentice Hall. 11a.m.-4p.m. every Wednesday from June 3 to Oct. 30.
Expect local farmers and market gardeners selling fruits, vegetables, herbs, honey, eggs, flowers, bread, and other prepared foods. These are great places to learn about new food. The Grown in Detroit Cooperative is on hand as well.

**East Warren Farmers Market (Saturday)**
At the northeast corner of Bishop Street and East Warren Avenue in Detroit; open 10 a.m. to 3 p.m. every Saturday starting June 13.
Featuring all Michigan-grown and urban produce as well as local arts and crafts. This is just the second year that this market will be available. Come out and support it. For more information e mail: eastwarrenavefarmersmarket@gmail.com

**Royal Oak Farmers Market (Saturdays & Sundays)**
At 316 E. 11 Mile Rd, Royal Oak. Open year-round! 7 a.m. – 1 p.m. Fridays, May through December. 7 a.m. – 1p.m. Saturdays, April through December. 8 a.m. – 2 p.m. Saturdays January through March. e mail: ci.royal-oak.mi.us/farmersmkt.
Plenty of local produce sold to you by the farmers year round. Take advantage!

**Birmingham Farmers' Market (Sundays)**
666 N. Old Woodward, in Public Parking Lot #6, across from Booth Park, Birmingham. June 7-October 25, 9 a.m. – 2 p.m. Sundays. e mail: birminghamfarmersmarket.org
Locally and regionally grown produce, including veggies and fruits. There are also children's activities, prepared foods, flowers and more. Make sure your license is straight and check it out one Sunday.

**Ann Arbor Farmers' Market**
315 Detroit St.
**Open Year Round**
7 a.m. – 3 p.m Wednesdays and Saturdays May through December
8 a.m.- 3 p.m. Saurday's January through April

The AA farmer's market has a really cool set up and its open year round. Many local farms, plants, crafts, and goodies are on the scene. It is a great way to spend a pretty fall afternoon in Michigan. Or anytime weekend you want to come out, as they are open year round for your convenience!

Check on the website **www.likeugiveadamn.com** for a more detailed listing. Ann Arbor, Dearborn, Farmington Hills, Mount Clemens, Saline, Chelsea, Rochester, Ortonville, and Plymouth also have farmers markets' seasonally.

The information is very easily accessible online.

The local produce is not only cheaper and fresher; it is also better for both you and our environment. Try to avoid the commercial grocer and deal directly with farms and farmers markets'.

Take a friend or family member and split the huge amounts of fresh food you get very affordably.

You will find farmers markets' are a much more pure way of doing business. No scanners and beeps as you get your food. Dealing directly with the grower is an experience you will never get at a grocery store.

# Chapter 5
# Family Owned Farms

The meat industry is absolutely out of control!

Industry farming is both unethical and unsanitary. The farms are disgusting. The animals are raised inhumanely—in absolutely horrible conditions. Anti-biotics have to be added to animals "feed" because of rampant disease. Doctors are now reporting that anti-biotic treatments are much less effective in people now as a result.

The animals are often literally born in cages, and kept crammed indoors until the slaughter. It is common that they never get to see the sun or touch the dirt. They eat a cheap synthetic "feed" as opposed to their natural diets.

WOW!! How inhumane is that?! Can you imagine that type of existence?

The employees, most of whom are underpaid immigrants by now, are often unqualified and mistreated. The whole thing has become a terrible, corporate, operation. THAT IS NOT A PLACE WHERE WE WANT TO GET FOOD FROM!!

Agricultural occupations are consistently rated some of the most dangerous jobs in America, and have the highest turnover rate. You DO NOT want to eat something coming from that awful energy! That energy goes inside your being.

The largest US slaughterhouses kill as many as 8.5 million birds in a week! In the US alone, 660,000 animals are killed per hour. The conditions in which the animals live under is absolutely ridiculous, yet fewer than one out of 250,000 animals get tested for toxic chemical residues. How can there be any discussion about where disease comes from?

Killing that number of animals is not natural!!! Not in line with nature, or whatever morality system that you own. How would God (Mother Nature) feel about that? Don't support those foul practices!

The farms listed here are not industrial farms. Their animals at least eat and graze naturally. Making them healthier.

These are old family farms that still take pride in their work; they have maintained respect for the dignity of the process. You are welcome to visit the farm and see how the animals are raised for yourself. Meet the actual farmers that raise the livestock you'll eat.

That is such a far cry from the cashier scanning your package of (so-called) "Amish" chicken parts.

That is a label that says Amish. You don't know where that chicken came from at all! It could be from a cloned chicken for all you know. Don't feed your family that unidentified, steroid filled meat.

These Michigan farms have delivery and pick-up options that are workable. For the peace of mind, it is certainly worth your time. If you are going to eat meat, it is in your best interest to go to a local, family owned farms.

Take control over what you are going to allow into your body. That step alone can ensure you a longer, healthier life, and a much better frame of mind.

Here are some of the local farms in Michigan. There are a lot of farms in this area.

To see a more complete listing, google: 'Organic farms in Michigan' and you will get a lot of links. (www.eatwild.com is a really good one.)

*Local Farm in Columbus, Michigan*

## Chapter 6
# Family Farms in Michigan

*Creswick Farms* is "dedicated to raising healthy, happy animals—lovingly cared for just as Mother Nature intended—which provide high energy, nutritious and delicious food sources for health-conscious individuals."

At Creswick Farms, we guarantee our animals are raised without antibiotics or growth hormones. This promise is your assurance that our products meet a higher standard for natural: they are truly naturally raised. The animals enjoy non-herbicide/chemical fertilized pasture and are supplied free choice with organic minerals and kelp. Our meats are processed in a family-owned slaughterhouse and are vacuum-packed to preserve freshness and improve shelf life.

Many families rely on us for their Beef, Pork, Turkey, Chicken and Eggs, and a large portion of our clientele reside in the Detroit and Chicago areas. We are located within a 2 ½ - 3 hour's drive of each city. For these customers we also have scheduled deliveries and pre-determined meeting points.

We always welcome visitors at our farm as we enjoy showing customers how our animals are nurtured to nurture us in the future. We especially enjoy children, who enjoy learning about the animals and their relationship to our food sources.

Our normal hours are between 9 a.m. and 5 p.m.

Please call or e-mail for informational brochure.

**Creswick Farms**
Andrea & Nathan Creswick
6500 Rollenhagen Road
Ravenna MI 49451
(616) 837-9226
E-mail: Creswick@altelco.net
Website: www.Creswickfarms.com

*Earth Shine Farm* is a small, sustainable, family-run farm that cuts no corners in providing healthy food, while treating our animals and the environment with the utmost respect.

Our Gourmet Heirloom Chickens are Barred Plymouth Rocks, the first breed admitted to the American Poultry Association well over 150 years ago. They look, behave, and taste like their ancestors did. In fact, they taste so deliciously different that one food writer claimed they shouldn't even be called chicken!

We raise our chickens on Michigan's Saginaw Valley pastures following the meticulous and humane French Label Rouge standards. They live on the natural delicacies they forage, along with certified-organic feed we grind fresh weekly to ensure maximum nutritional value. We set our birds out immediately, not even waiting a week before introducing them to grass, where they remain for a *minimum* of 84 days. They're processed on-farm using the 'air chill' method that not only yields a superior product, but is also *cleaner*, less *contamination-prone*, and more e*nvironmentally sound.*

Unless you're over a century-and-a-half old (and if so, kudos!), we believe you've never tasted chicken like ours. Purebred Barred Rocks like ours are a rare bird indeed. They don't grow on trees, but they sure love to roost in 'em.

Visit our website and see what some truly great chefs and gourmands have to say about Earth Shine Farm Chickens. We ship fresh-frozen.

**Earth Shine Farm**
Frank & Laura Kay Jones
9580 New Lothrop Road
Durand MI 48429.
(989) 288-2421.
E-mail: earthshinefarm@gmail.com
Website: http://www.earthshinefarm.com

*Garden Patch Farm* is a small family-owned and operated Certified Naturally Grown farm—no chemicals of any kind. (www.naturallygrown.org) *No GMOS, pesticides, chemical fertilizers, herbicides, hormones, vaccines, antibiotics, or animal by-products!* We work hard to provide nutritious food you can feel good about eating.

Now taking orders for Certified organic grass fed beef by the 1/8th, 1/4, 1/2 and whole, only $4.50/lb! Visit our website for details.

Starting March 8th, we will offer Certified organic grass fed beef by the cut from Graham's Organic farm! You will be able to purchase steak, roasts, hamburger, liver, heart, tongue, and soup bones while supplies last.

Certified Organic Pastured Roasting Chickens available on our farm from Graham's Organic Farm, only $3.69/lb. Call us for yours today!

Certified Naturally Grown pastured chicken eggs. Our chickens feed on untreated grasses, sweet clovers, and bugs in our pastures. Additionally, they eat certified organic grains and fresh water daily.

Eggs year-round, self-serve from the fridge on the front porch of our house—pay by the honor system.

We also offer raw honey, raw sauerkraut, sprouted spelt flour, sprouted kamut flour, and sprouted cream of spelt cereal. The flours are all certified organic. Visit our website for details on products and hours of operation.

**Garden Patch Farm**
Tim and Robin Leonard
1523 East M-36
Pinckney, MI 48169
(734) 878-2920
E-mail: robin@gardenpatchfarm.com
Website: http://www.gardenpatchfarm.com

*Happy Hill Farm* began raising chickens and turkeys on pasture in 1999. We are committed to moving them to fresh grass every day. We put them outside as soon as the babies are able to handle the out-of-doors, usually at 2–3 weeks, and keep them outside all the rest of their lives. Laying hens go inside for the winter when it starts to snow but go back out as soon as the snow is gone. We try to give them hay through the winter. We try to take care of the land as we feel God would want us to, with no synthetic chemicals.

We have a small farm store where we sell fresh poultry through the summer and frozen year round. We offer any cuts of chicken or turkey you might want, including turkey sausage, ground turkey, boneless skinless breast meat, and all the other parts, as well as whole birds. We do all the processing and packaging on-farm with the help of our children.

We also offer some produce in the summer. We just completed a large greenhouse and hope to soon offer fresh salad greens year-round. We will be offering CSA subscriptions in the spring for summer crops or in the fall for salad stuff over the winter.

**Happy Hill Farm**
Emma Filbrun
2878 East Scout Road, Hart MI 49420.
(231) 873-8972.
E-mail: happyhillfarmgf@yahoo.com

*A Pear fresh off of the tree, only at Eastern Market. Bought from the farmer who grew it.*

*Sunshine Meadows Farm* is a small, family farm utilizing organic practices in raising our food and animals. We have a mixed flock of chickens and sell brown, green, white and chocolate eggs in mixed dozens, year-round.

Our chickens enjoy spending their days out on pasture that is free from pesticides and herbicides, with lots of bugs and tidbits to eat. They choose to roost in their coop when the sun sets at night which protects them from predators. Grains that are free of by-products, antibiotics or hormones is offered free choice. Spring of 2008 we will be transitioning to 100% organic grain to supplement their pastured diet. Fall of 2008 should see the addition of duck eggs, too.

Chickens eggs are $3/dozen. Also available from May-September 2008 is a variety of vegetables grown in an organic method.

Check out our web site for availability updates or feel free to call/email. Hours vary, so please call/e-mail first so we don't miss you! Closed Sunday.

**Sunshine Meadows Farm**
**Lorij and David Schmick**
**2610 Cook Trail, Ortonville MI 48462**
**(248) 464-1825**
E-mail: lorij@sunshinemeadowsfarm.com ✉
Website: http://www.sunshinemeadowsfarm.com

*Middleton Berry Farm*—raspberries, strawberries, tomatoes, sweet corn, peppers and pumpkins
4888 Oakwood Road
Ortonville, MI 48462
Phone: 248-628-1819
Email: middletonberryfarm@yahoo.com.
Crops are usually available in:
June, July, August, September, and October.
Open: Call for picking days and times
Payment: Cash, Check.

## Chapter 7
# *Reading is Fundamental*

Perhaps the most important concept in this handbook pertains to reading the labels of EVERYTHING that you are going to eat.

Every bottle, package, or container has the ingredients listed in order of volume. Examine that list and scrutinize everything you are going to allow inside of your body.

We teach our children not to take candy from a stranger, we should also teach them to know what they are putting inside their bodies at all times. That is important as well! We cannot just trust things the way we used to, it is a different world we live in now.

A lot of people stop at the black & white chart. The chart does have valid information, but it is often misleading. That is not where you want to focus. You want to peep the ingredients. You are what you eat. Know what you are putting inside your temple. Everything.

That is how you determine whether or not you should be consuming a product. An easy, and wise rule to follow is if you can't read it (without a dictionary)—then don't eat it! It is that simple.

If upon examining a products contents, you find it is some chemical crap that you cannot even pronounce, why would you want to put that inside your body? If you are confused trying to read it, it's a good chance your body gets confused trying to digest it! That leads to imbalance and blockages in your system.

This is the information age, why not use that to your advantage? Go through your kitchen RIGHT NOW and take out some of your products and read them. Google anything on there that looks foreign to you, and you will see why it is important to stay aware of what's inside of your everyday products. Those ingredients will become a part of your temple.

*Read the fine print.*

## *Human Lab Rats*

Today people are eating more processed foods than ever before in history. There is also more diseases than ever before in history. Coincidence?

How much DISODIUM INOSINATE or SODIUM CASEINATE or MALTODEXTRIN, YELLOW # 6, or RED # 40 do you think your system can ingest without some type of adverse effect on your body? Not long.

Those are not natural substances. They do not come from the ground where food grows—those things come from a laboratory. If you keep eating laboratory creations, as opposed to nature's gifts, you will surely end up needing laboratory drugs and medicines.

That is the vicious cycle here in America.

We have to try to eat more fresh foods from the ground, and less stuff that comes from cans, boxes, bags, and packages.

A **bag of chips** is a common snack. Nobody is implying that chips are the devil—rather illustrating where you need to make better decisions regarding what you are going to allow inside your body (temple).

For example, here is a list of what is in a *popular* brand of chips that you see at every store, everyday. (One which I used to love as a child too!! I would lick the stuff off of both sides, then eat it. But I didn't know or care what the "stuff" was, I am thankful that I have evolved.):

**INGREDIENTS: WHOLE CORN, VEGETABLE OIL (CONTAINS ONE OR MORE OF THE FOLLOWING: CORN, SOYBEAN, AND/OR SUNFLOWER OIL), SALT, CHEDDAR CHEESE (CULTURED MILK, SALT, ENZYMES), MALTODEXTRIN, WHEAT FLOWER, WHEY, MONOSODIUM GLUTAMATE, BUTTERMILD SOLIDS, ROMANO CHEESE FROM COWS MILK (PART-SKIM COW'S MILK, CHEESE CULTURES, SALT, ENZYMES), WHEY PROTEIN CONCENTRATE, ONION POWDER, PARTIALLY HYDROGENATED SOYBEAN AND COTTONSEED OIL, CORN FLOUR, DISODIUM PHOSPHATE, LACTOSE, NATURAL AND ARTIFICIAL FLAVORS, DEXTROSE, TOMATO POWDER, SPICES, LACTIC ACID, ARTIFICIAL COLOR (INCLUDING YELLOW 6, YELLOW 5, RED 40), CITRIC ACID, SUGAR, GARLIC POWDER, RED AND GREEN BELL PEPPER POWDER, SODIUM CASEINATE, DISODIUM INOSINATE, DISODIUM GUANNYOATEK, NONFAT MILK SOLIDS, WHEY PROTEIN ISOLATE, AND CORN SYRUP SOLIDS. CONTAINS MILK AND WHEAT INGREDIENTS.**

*(Of course HFCS AND Partially Hydrogenated Oils are illegal in other parts of the world)*

All of that stuff is in one bag of chips? That is absolutely crazy!! But who pays any attention to the list of ingredients? We generally stop at the chart with calories, grams of sugar, fat, etc. - without giving proper attention to the fine print, the ingredients.

How many of those things are laboratory creations? How does all of that stuff react going inside of my body at the same time? Who knows?

I would go out on a limb and say that a person eating that type of stuff as a snack regularly, is much more likely to develop serious health problems, than someone snacking on an apple or some grapes. I would bet the (local) farm on that. (LOL… a little vegan humor).

If you want some chips that are a little better to snack on, go to your local health food store. You will find snacks with much less harmful chemical content which cost relatively the same.

**For instance, this is a list of ingredients from a similar tortilla style chip from a health market:**

INGREDIENTS: CORN CHIPS, VEGETABLE OIL (CONTAINS ONE OR MORE OF THE FOLLOWING) SUNFLOWER/SAFFLOWER AND/OR SOYBEAN OIL), SEA SALT.

That's it.

That is a brand of tortilla chips, which taste pretty similar to the popular brand. There are several kinds for you to explore. All kinds of flavors—and they are all made with a conscious consumer in mind. Just comparing those two products—you can clearly see which one is a better choice for your overall health!! There is no question.

The types of things you and your family may be snacking on everyday can prove to be detrimental in the long run. Children today are getting more serious dis-eases at younger ages than ever before. We can most certainly point to things like the increase of processed foods being a large factor in that.

It is more important now than ever that we utilize our resources. Read the labels of anything that we are going to put inside our bodies. Google something if you are unsure what it is. Take that time for you and your family's health.

You have to read even the things that you might take for granted. Of course we never really thought about reading the ingredients back in the day. Who did?

This is a new era. ***IT IS IMPERATIVE TO TEACH YOUR CHILDREN TO READ THE INGREDIENTS FROM NOW ON!***

Randomly I picked up a "Nutri-Grain Cereal Bar". On the front the package boasts that it has "more of the whole grains your body needs." Here's what it really is:

INGREDIENTS: FILLING (**High Fructose Corn Syrup**, Corn Syrup, Blueberry Puree Concentrate, Glycerin, <u>Sugar</u>, Water, **Sodium Alginate**, Modified Corn Starch, **Natural and Artificial Flavors**, Citric Acid, **Methylcellulose, Dicalcium Phosphate**, Malic Acid, **Red #40, Blue #1**) Whole Grain Rolled Oats, Enriched Flour (Wheat Flour, Niacin, Reduced Iron, Thiamin Mononitrate (Vitamin B1), Riboflavin (Vitamin B2), Folic Acid) Whole Wheat Flour, Sunflower and/or Soybean Oil With **TBHQ** for freshness, **High Fructose Corn Syrup, Sugar**, Contains 2% or Less of Honey, **<u>Dextrose</u>**, Calcium Carbonate, Soluble Corn Fiber, Nonfat Dry Milk, Wheat Bran, Salt, Cellulose, Potassium Bicarbonate (Leavening), **Natural and Artificial Flavor, Mono—AND Diglycerides, Propelyne Glycol Esters of Fatty Acids, Soy Lecithin, Wheat Gluten**, Niacinamide, **Sodium Stearoyl Lactylate, Vitami**n A Palminate, **<u>Carrageenan</u>**, Zinc Oxide, Reduced Iron, Gaur Gum, pyridoxine Hydrochloride (Vitamin B6), Thiamin Hydrochloride (Vitamin B1), Riboflavin (B2), Folic Acid. Contains Wheat, Milk and Soy Ingredients.

What? Your body does NOT need all of that! You cannot simply read the packaging and think that something is good based on that alone!

It might have been safer to assume that products were ok 25 years ago. But today that mentality has to change. The products are no longer made with people's best interest in mind. It is huge business now.

Compare that to a fruit smoothie for breakfast. You'd do much better to find a brand of bar like that at a health food store, which won't have all the extra stuff inside it. Avoid garbage where you can.

You'd think a jar of peanut butter is pretty good for you. One would consider that a healthy snack for children. Now that you are a label reader—*<u>understand that you have to re-establish your position on everything</u>*. Commercial peanut butters are not actually good at all.

**(THE LEADING BRAND) PEANUT BUTTER "*EXTRA CRUNCHY*)"**

**INGREDIENTS:** MADE FROM ROASTED PEANUTS AND SUGAR, CONTAINS 2% OR LESS OF: MOLASSES, **<u>PARTIALLY HYDROGENATED VEGETABLE OIL (SOYBEAN), FULLY HYDROGENATED VEGETABLE OILS (RAPESEED AND SOYBEAN), MONO AND DIGLYCERIDES AND SALT.</u>**

Or maybe you want less fat in your peanut butter.

The Leading Brand PEANUT BUTTER "REDUCED FAT"

Ingredients: PEANUTS, CORN SYRUP SOLIDS, SUGAR AND SOY PROTEIN, CONTAINS 2% OR LESS OF: **FULLY HYDROGENATED VEG-**

**ETABLE OILS (RAPESEED AND SOYBEAN)**, SALT, **MONO- AND DI-GLYCERIDES**, MOLASSES, NIACINAMIDE, FOLIC ACID, **PYRIDOXINE HYDROCHLORIDE, MAGNESIUM OXIDE, ZINC OXIDE, FERRIC ORTHOPHOSPHATE**, AND COPPER

**PEANUT BUTTER.** So the natural kind might be a dollar or two more. But I think its well worth it. The bottom line is you want a product without dangerous Hydrogenated Oils, which is illegal in various parts of the world. Keep these things away from your family, giving your body a chance to maintain proper health.

## *Organic Peanut Butter*

**INGREDIENTS:** ORGANIC ROASTED PEANUTS, ROASTED PEANUT OIL, CONTAINS 1% OR LESS OF SALT.

*(There are many natural versions of peanut butter. Inspect and be aware of what is inside even the most common thing like peanut butter. It doesn't have to be "organic", you want things as natural as possible. Local perhaps. Peanuts, oil, and a little salt should be all that's necessary for peanut butter.)

*Real choosey moms **read labels**.*

Read everything from now on and avoid all that chemical stuff that going inside your body.

Don't support the corporations that are flooding the market with products that have cheap, dangerous ingredients inside. (KRAFT, HEINZ, GENERAL MILLS, NABISCO, ETC.) Those companies' market products to your children that are laced with ingredients that are really not safe for their consumption.

Even things that you may consider healthier snacks, (i.e. Wheat Thins, Golden Grahams, Peanut Butter Crackers, etc.) may have MANY questionable ingredients inside them! Read those boxes before you give those snacks to your children.

It is left up to you to become more aware and NOT support those types of products. Don't support the huge marketplaces that have consistently carried that garbage either.

Eat as much fresh fruit and food as possible for snacks. Learn to live without the microwave, get rid of it!

Bake cakes from scratch with your children. Learn together how to bake things dairy-free that are still warm and delicious.

Try hooking up some homemade jams, ice creams, popsicles, and smoothies—create things in your own kitchen. (Recipes will be listed on the website.)

*For help regarding what to watch out for on labels, check out www.truthinlabeling.org.*

*Fresh fruit and squeezed juice is as sweet as any candy!!*

# Chapter 8

# *Everyday Suicide*

*IT IS TIME THAT WE WAKE UP!!!*

You are eating something EVERY SINGLE DAY of your life that is very harmful to your system. It has been proven many times over to be very dangerous. In fact, many feel that it is largely responsible for rise of obesity in this country.

How dangerous is it? In European countries, which have universal health care, the governments made HFCS **ILLEGAL** for use in ANY food product. *Banned* it. After reviewing the medical findings, they determined it was lethal and banned it from any food or beverage products in their country.

Read this slow and think about it: **In European countries (and Canada), where health care is provided by the government, they determined it was lethal and disallowed its use in any food. IT IS ILLEGAL FOR A COMPANY TO MAKE A PRODUCT USING THIS SUBSTANCE AT ALL.**

*ILLEGAL!! Over 10 years ago!*

Here in the United States, where we have commercials advertising "new" drugs, where private health care is a huge business, it is in nearly EVERY PRODUCT on the shelves of your local 'super' market. Nearly 90% of the products in your grocery store are filled with the sh*t.

## *High Fructose Corn Syrup*

Google it.

That should tell you a couple of things.

The health care industry in America is huge business. They know how dangerous a substance HFCS is. They have to. But they also know what kind of money they make in drug$ & medicine$. That is THE biggest industry in America.

It is in this country's best interest to keep people sick. That way they can sell us pills. Why bother with trying to keep people healthy, and out of the pharmacies? That would be taking away from the pot.

I can't put it any better than Rory Freedman and Kim Barnouin in their best selling book Skinny Bitch, Chapter 9, "Have No Faith: The Government Agencies don't give a s#*& about your health!"

They really don't.

That is something that you have to come to grips with. It is hard (for some) to accept that. Some people feel like "they" wouldn't do that to us—I guess that is how some people insist on thinking.

Do some quick research on your own. You will see that the government agencies do very little to protect us from the food industry. They are often in cahoots with one another.

But you also remember who controls the media. You may see some articles in support of the HFCS. Propaganda machine. They even had those COMMERCIALS airing about it a while back!!

Unbelievable.

Look for any unbiased press, medical research, and decide for yourself. It was certainly strong enough concern for European countries to ban it OVER 10 YEARS AGO. (I don't want it in my temple!)

High Fructose Corn Syrup was introduced in the early 80's. By the mid 80's the sweetener gained popularity all over the world. Several years' later reports of many negative health issues started coming from everywhere.

HFCS is linked directly with the rise of the obesity rate in America and abroad. It was reported that the sweetener also promotes conditions such as type 2 diabetes, high blood pressure and coronary artery disease—such disorders continue to soar in the US today.

Why would the US continue to overuse something that has that kind of track record? **_GREED!_** (Of course.)

Sugar cane must be imported; it only grows in tropical climates of South America & Africa. But corn, it grows right here in the good ole U S of A. So naturally, a process to make a sweetener out of corn is very appealing to our government. We have plenty of corn; it is dirt cheap to produce despite its noted dangers.

Extra taxes are put on company's that are importing sugar cane, making it alluring for companies to use this dangerous substance instead.

It is processed even more than white sugar. It is actually sweeter than sugar after processing. So it can be bought in smaller capacity. Another big draw for food manufactures is the fact that HFCS HAS A SHELF LIFE OF 7 YEARS OR MORE. It is both a sweetener AND a preservative. So it is cheaper to use and after its packaged, it will taste the same for nearly a decade.

Not to mention it's going to keep the customers coming to get medicines and drugs! That is a win-win for America.

*And a lose-lose for you!*

You have to take the initiative of taking care of you and your family's future health.

This generation is eating more packaged, processed food than any one before. That is setting the stage for major health concerns in the very near future if we don't make better health decisions.

Let's start the transition today!

Your body is a temple. ***EAT LIKE YOU GIVE A DAMN!***

*This is when you want to have your reading glasses on. Your body is a blessing—you should care to know what you are putting inside.*

## Where is High Fructose Corn Syrup?
*Where isn't it?*

It is in ALL Pops & Soda's. ALL OF THEM! All Pepsi, Coke, Faygo products—ALL U.S. sodas are sweetened and preserved with HFCS.

It is in nearly all bottled beverages that you might see at a gas station or party store including:

**Gatorade**—which is supposedly for athletes. *Drink water instead.*

**Vitamin Water**—which "sounds" healthy for you, is laced with HFCS; Drink water and take a liquid vitamin.

**Everfresh Juices**—the little glass bottles have HFCS.

**Arizona Iced Teas**—brew your own teas. These have HFCS inside. Even simple Ice tea!

Just to name a few bottled drinks. Start picking up the bottle and reading it. You will find it is in everything! I GUARANTEE if you shop at any major chain grocer (Farmer Jack, Kroger, Miejers), there is HFCS in nearly every packaged thing in your refrigerator & cabinet.

The average person is EASILY consuming HFCS several times on a daily basis.

*That is scary to me! That is something we have to cut out immediately!*

It is in most commercial brand products.

**Ketchup**—HFCS is the second ingredient listed in Heinz or any commercial ketchup. (Any Heinz product).

**Barbeque Sauce**—THE first ingredient listed in Open Pit!! (ingredients, of course, are listed by volume)

*It is in almost all condiments*

**A1 Steak Sauce**

**Mayonnaises**

**Commercial Salad Dressings**

It is in ALL of those little snacks you are giving your children.

**Cheez itz**

**Peanut butter crackers**

**Ritz cracker snacks**

**Graham Crackers**

**Animal Crackers**

It is even in stuff that you may consider healthy like:

Wheat Thins, some Wheat breads, Bagels, Ice Cream, some Tomato sauces, etc. You name it!!

When I say it is in **EVERYTHING**. I *mean* it. Start reading ingredients! You will see that HFCS is in almost EVERYTHING in a box, package, or bottle at the commercial grocery store. That is why I implore you NOT to shop there.

Just going to a healthy store or marketplace, you start to learn different approaches, find new products and things to replace the junk that is sold by big corporations. Start to educate yourself by simply going to the proper venues.

You will find a snack exactly just like Cheez its—without HFCS or dangerous Hydrogenated Oils (Which are also ILLEGAL IN EUROPEAN COUNTRIES.) Find the similar type of products, like Graham crackers, but without all the dangerous ingredients.

Simply get all of your sauces, condiments, and dressings free of all the chemicals & preservatives, and of course free of HFCS. You are only going to be able to do that at a health conscious market.

Start changing by getting the better type products from now on. Eventually you want to grow towards making all of your own fresh sauces and condiments. Put your energy, love, and creativity inside it. That is the way you want to nourish your temple.

***Stay out of the grocery store! That is the perfect way to start to unplug.***

Do not even go there and try to get the "healthy" stuff. Shopping there supports the garbage that they peddle to everyone in the community. Don't support a venue filled with 90% corporate trash food, even if they have a small 'organic' section.

They set that up for **business**. They are still doing way more harm than good.

What you can't get from a farm, or farmer's/fruit market—get at a smaller store that is dedicated to having health minded products all the time. You might have to pay a little more at a health store. But remember it is for you temple.

Also keep in mind that it is but a step in the process. The next step is going to be thinking of producing instead of always consuming. That is the healthiest and most cost effective way off all.

There is much more on all of this in volume 2. Stay tuned. But start to make your transition NOW!

Transform your kitchen and home to a safer place.

Eating better does not mean that you have to sacrifice flavor. Its not all nasty. There are alternatives that taste just as good, while still being much better for you.

Try some of these items in your home as you begin to make a conscious effort towards experiencing a healthier existence.

*(Refer to the shopping tips to show you exactly where to get these items,)*

*An idea of what a tasty, healthier breakfast choice looks like. Even some commercial Bagels have HFCS and other questionable ingredients. Read everything you are going to eat.*

## Chapter 9
# *If You Like This…Try This*

*Country Crock or Margarine*                                                              *Soy Butter*

This is a very easy transition. Non-dairy Soy Butter taste exactly the same and it is better for you. It has no cholesterol and you avoid dairy! The cost is very comparible to Country Crock or whatever you use now. Use extra virgin olive oil instead of butter when you can too.

*Pops/Juice/Gatorade*                                                       *Water*
                                                                                                *Herbal Teas*

Remember water is essential to life. Trying to drink 8 glasses a day will keep you pretty full. Drinking all of those sugar filled liquids deprive the body of water and do not quench the bodies thirst for fresh water. Plus the majority of them have HFCS, artificial colors, and flavors. Even Gatorade and Vitamin Water, look at the ingredients. Water is what you should be drinking (try for a gallon a day!) to help keep you healthy—the body is able to flush out toxins and flow naturally. Herbal tea not only tastes good and its medicinal. You don't want those Arizona cans or bottles of Iced Tea. That is full of junk as well. Brew your own tea and ice it for the family.

*Sour Cream*                                                                                    *Toffuti Sour Cream*

Another dairy product that can be replaced with a non-dairy substitute, but the Toffuti stuff is no mere substitute. It is good for real! People I know who LOVE sour cream had no problems switching to Toffuti. It contains ZERO cholesterol, doesn't create the same mucus in the system, and is much better for you. It costs relatively the same.

*Cream Cheese*                                                                    *Toffuti Cream Cheese*

Yet another dairy product replacement. Use it on your bagel instead of Philadelphia Cream Cheese. Less mucus, NO cholesterol, AND it taste the same if not better than cream cheese!! Seriously. (This should be the "real" kind, and Philly brand should be the "fake" one. Switch your mentality about things).

*Skip/Jiffy/etc Peanut Butter*                                       *Organic Peanut Butter*

Commercial brand peanut butters contain a lot of sugar and sodium. They also use harmful Hydrogenated Oils, and some of them have High Fructose Corn Syrup in them as well.

This is where you have to read these labels. Peanut butter IS *NOT JUST* peanut butter! Jiff, Skippy, and all of those are commercial brands are highly processed garbage. There is a *huge* difference in the two products. Go read the bottles and you will see.

The better kinds might costs a little more, but you avoid those harmful ingredients. So many people look at Peanut Butter as healthy, but that commercial brand stuff is pure GARBAGE! DO NOT feed that to your children. The same goes for those little peanut butter crackers and what not too.

Spend the extra dollar or two and get a brand you can feel good about. WholeFoods or Rocky Peanut Company have peanut butter fresh made on site, with just peanuts and oil. No other crap inside. Remember to try to eat as fresh as possible. Strive to get everything you can with NO preservatives or additives. READ THE INGREDIENTS!

~~*Doritos/Cheetos/etc.*~~  *Tortilla chips* (*Flax seed or Local*)
*Kettle chips* (*salt and pepper*)

Look at the list of ingredients on a bag of Doritos or Cheetos. It looks like you need a science degree to read and understand most of that stuff. Why would you want to eat that?! It is not natural at all. If you look at some of these other brands, like the Trader Joe brands, or those at Natural Food Patch—you will see much less long words and many more things you recognize. No red #40 or blue #10 or whatever. Eat food, not chemicals.

~~*Coffee*~~  *Guarana Coffee* (*A Healthy Coffee*)
*Yerba Matte or Black Teas*

If you are an avid coffee drinker, try to replace that with a strongly steeped cup of Yerba Matte or Black Tea every now and again. That might give you a burst of energy, some natural caffeine, but not as hard on the system as coffee. Once you have cleansed and get the long scientific words out of your diet, you won't need anything for energy. You are going to wake up ready to go!

~~*Heinz Ketchup*~~  *Organic Ketchup*

Heinz ketchup, which sits on the table of restaurants all over the place, is of course laced with high fructose corn syrup. (I know Heinz has an organic brand that (supposedly) does not contain HFCS, but I frankly do not choose to support a company that has used the dangerous ingredient for so long! They care more about profit and a "health trend" than they do about your children's health.) Organic

Ketchups tastes the same. I have done taste tests! You cannot tell the difference, but your body definitely can. Try it. There are several brands available at your local health food store.

### *Mayonnaise*                                                                                      *Veganaise*

Mayonnaise has dairy and eggs inside, yet it sits out warm on the shelves. Something is wrong with that. Start picking up the jar and reading it instead of just buying it. Veganaise taste so much the same ($4.59 a jar at Natural Food Patch) that I don't even like it! It contains absolutely NO CHOLESTEROL; the commercial brands are loaded with it! Why not get the healthier alternative?

### *Open Pit Barbeque Sauce*                                      *Natural BBQ Sauce*

Those bottles of Open Pit are nothing but High Fructose, sugar, and salt. No wonder it tastes good. It is no good for you. Find a brand that has no HFCS and less sugar. You have to go to a health food store and pick things up and read the labels. You will see the difference. You will feel the difference in your body. Do this with all your staple items. DO NOT shop at commercial grocers, save-a-lot's, or Dollar stores for these types of items—or you will get heavily processed, preserved, dangerous products. Its that simple. If your thinking about the cost, meat is the bulk of most grocery bills. Leave the meat, which is quite dangerous too, out of the equation. Then you will have an extra dollar or two to keep the healthier products in your home.

### *Lawry's Seasoning Salt*                                         *Non-Salt seasoning salt*
                                                                                      *Liquid Amino's*
                                                                                                           *Sea Salt*

Everybody has that big thing of Lawry's in the crib! Throw it out! Stray away from using salt at all. Especially a processed salt like that. Sea salt, while it is processed, is thought to be much better for you than traditional iodized table salt.

    They also make Non-Salt seasoning salt, and a host of other alternatives. That is why you go to a health minded store. You will start to find healthier replacements for everything, and you can read the label to determine exactly why. It will enhance your transition. Liquid Amino's have a naturally salty taste, you can spray that on things to add a healthy salty twist.

    Start to think about seasoning your food with fresh peppers, garlic, ginger, cilantro, and various herbs—use more fresh ingredients to season your food. Be creative.

*Sugar*                                                      *Maple Syrup*
*Raw Honey*
*Agave Nectar*

In the last 20 years, we have increased sugar consumption in the U.S. from 26 pounds to 135 lbs. of sugar per person per year!* Sugar not only causes behavioral problems in children, (and adults!) it also depresses the immune system. We know how diabetes has risen, especially in young people. Fungus' also thrive on sugar and it upsets the mineral balance in the body. There are too many reasons to list to get OFF of sugar. Google 'dangers of sugar' and think it over. Agave syrup, pure Maple syrup, or raw honey should replace sugar in your diet. *Right now!*

*White Flour*                              *Whole Wheat Flour*
*Soy Flour*
*Coconut Flour*

White flour is just as dangerous as sugar! Try to avoid it. There are alternatives like Whole Wheat Flour, Soy Flour, and Coconut Flour, which are better choices as they have some natural fiber and nutrient content. Look for that in your breads and baked goods. Remember you are a label reader now!!

*Aunt Jemima Syrup*                                *Maple Syrup*
*Commercial Brand Syrup*

The very first ingredient of its list is High Fructose Corn Syrup! It consists of more HFCS than water!! So you know it is no good for you. Maple Syrup again has nutritional value and is sweet flavored. It really cost a lot more, but it is well worth it. Avoid eating that dangerous sweetener when you can.

*Eggs*                                                             *Tofu Scramble*

Tofu scramble is really just like eggs, of course, without the "I'm eating an infant chicken" thing going on. (Sunday morning breakfast at the Golden Gate is a great place to try it, and enjoy the peaceful vibe.) It is really good with potatoes and veggie sausage.

*Huge Commercial Grocers*                     *Smaller Health Food Store*
*Farmer's Market*
*Local Farm*
*Your yard, porch*

I hope by now you are seeing the pattern here. The things sold at the large chain stores are simply products in a huge industry. It is business driven and not made

*\* thehealingdaily.com*

with your health in mind.

Tyson chicken has an industry system, where chickens are mere products; machines kill and chop the poor birds into neat packages. It has gotten way out of control.

8.5 million birds in a single week! Imagine that. As a people, we are getting farther and farther away from the natural ways of living. (We are destroying the environment and killing ourselves as a result.)

Make better choices for yourself and your family. Take the time to know where your food is coming from, support the local, family farms where you know there is still some integrity left in the process.

The commercial brands at large stores are full of high fructose corn syrup, artificial colors and flavors, cholesterol, and preservatives. You cannot find healthy options in that type of store. NONE of the snacks are healthy.

*Liquid Aminos can help to replace iodized salt. Here are some of the many natural BBQ Sauce and Ketchup options. Eventually start thinking about making those things inside your home as well. That is the direction you want to flow: From the commercial brands, to the "good kinds", to making condiments at home—where you know exactly what is inside it for sure.*

The meat sold there is shot up with all type of chemicals, steroids, dyes and antibiotics. You have no idea what that package of meat has been through before it reaches that store shelf.

## Dairy Milk

*Rice Milk*
*Soy Milk*
*Almond Milk*

Dairy cows are artificially inseminated all year round so that they keep producing milk. Their udders are mechanically squeezed. Blood, puss, frustration and all goes into the mix. Don't drink that misery. The alternatives taste very similar to milk without the inhumane history. Cow's milk contains hormones that are designed for baby cow's, not human beings! Allergies, Asthma, and sinus problems have all been linked directly to today's dairy products.

## Meats

*Tofurkey Sausages/Meats*
*Non-Chicken Strips*
*Veggie Burgers*
*Seitan*
*Tempeh*

How do you replace meat? **Veggie burgers** can be good with grilled onions, on an onion roll, or an Avalon bun. You won't miss the cholesterol and blood of beef at all!! Add soy cheese and make it a cheeseburger. **Black bean burgers**, **Eggplant burgers**, **Portabella Mushroom burgers**—marinated and prepared right, they can all be delicious! Making things at home ensures that you and your family won't have so many mystery chemical ingredients going into your systems on a daily basis.

Instead of frying pork sausage in the morning, try some of the replacement stuff. Little non-sausage patties taste just as good (with tofu scramble) as scrambled eggs and sausage does. Really. Plus you won't be eating a filthy hog to start your day. You have to open yourself up to things in which you might not be accustomed.

**Tofurkey** Sausage is an excellent transition food. They have several flavors to try and they taste just like meat. They are perfect for cookouts instead of Italian sausage or Bratwurst—throw on some Tofurkeys in those same flavors. Introduce these kinds of things to your family.

You are going to hear jokes and whatever because people are immature about it. Stop feeding the kids those damn nasty hot dogs! That is the scrap meat of diseased animals! It is way past time that we reinvent the whole "ribs and soul food" thing. We are literally eating ourselves to death and JOKING about it. We have to become more conscious as a community. This is a very serious thing.

(Trader Joes) **Chicken-less strips** are good as chicken replacements. Especially on salads, Fajitas, Tacos and things like that. They have beef replacement strips as well. That is a good way for you to begin to transition towards healthier life choices.

**Tempeh** is another chicken strip replacement. It is high in protein, low in cholesterol, a good thing to introduce to your family. **Seitan** is a good beef replacement in stews and such, with meat like consistency. Tofu can also top your stir-fry type of dishes as well. Be open and creative—and most of all healthy.

If some of these dishes are totally foreign to you, it would be a good idea to go to a vegetarian restaurant in your area that knows how to hook it up already. You can learn what you like that way, and get a better idea of how to make it. AJ's Music Café has a Seitan Reuben sandwich that is wonderful. If you can learn to make that you won't even miss Lou's Deli.

You can make "turkey" subs, or "salami" sandwiches with Tofurkey lunchmeat, and people won't be able to tell the difference. Once you start learning how to prepare things, the transition gets easier and easier.

You will be feeling better the whole time too!

Of course some fabulous recipes will be demonstrated for you on the website. www.likeugiveadamn.com

*Quinoa, cooked with fresh tomatoes and green peppers. Served with Avocado. This is a complete high protein meal with no chicken breast or egg whites. You can try something like this after a workout. Its light and digest easily.*

## *Don't look at eating healthy as a handicap!*

Understand that you can still make your fabulous dinner recipes, snacks, and sweets inside your home. You can still love to eat, and enjoy food! Just be creative.

Remember to think towards producing things as opposed to always being a consumer. Your goal should be to assume total control over what is going inside your temple.

Make better choices. Cookies you bake from scratch at home are made with such better energy than a package of "Chips-a-Hoy", or whatever you buy at the local grocer or gas station. Making things at home keeps your family away from many chemicals going into your system on a daily basis.

Mass production and profit are the goals behind those products, not love and health. Those are machine made and packaged snacks!

## *How far is that from your own hands and loving energy?*

Love has a nutritional value that mass production simply cannot replace. Ignore that mystery Hostess crap, which you know is full of chemicals and junk. Make your food, snacks, and treats at home as much as possible.

## *Make it vegan!*

We just have to get accustomed to safer ways to prepare things. With a little education and substitution you can bake, cook, and live a vegan lifestyle quite easily. And most importantly, you will feel better than ever while you do it!

| *If it calls for this:* | *Use This:* |
| --- | --- |
| 1-cup sugar | 1-cup raw cane sugar |
| 1-cup of cow milk | 1-cup soy/rice/almond |
| 1-cup buttermilk | 1-cup soy milk* (add 2 tsp lemon juice or white vinegar) |
| 1-cup yogurt | 1-cup soy yogurt |
| 1 oz cheese | 1 oz. dairy-free cheese |
| 1-cup cottage cheese | 1-cup mashed tofu* (firm) |
| 1 cup cream cheese | 1-cup mashed tofu* (Drained medium works well) |
| 1-cup Ricotta cheese (as in lasagna) | 1-cup mashed tofu* (Firm works well) |
| 1-cup ice cream | 1-cup frozen soy/rice dessert |
| 1-cup whipping cream | 12 oz firm tofu + 1 cup maple Syrup + Tbsp lemon juice + 1 tsp vanilla, blended** |

Moo Moo's Vegetarian Cuisine, an affordable local company that is founded on making quality vegan/vegetarian foods. This is the kind of company you want to support as their products are actually made with your families health in mind..

*from *Becoming Vegan,* Brenda Davis, R.D. & Vesanto Melina, M.S., R.D. Book Publishing Company, Tenessee)
** from *Cooking Vegetarian*, V, Melina, J. Forest, Wiley/Macmillan Canada

# Chapter 10
# The Smooth(ie) Way to Healthy Lifestyle

Smoothies are an excellent way to get a lot of vitamins and nutrients inside your system effectively, in one delicious tasting drink. Select a combination of fruits, (i.e blueberry, cherry, blackberry) some ice, water, and Agave Nectar or Maple Syrup. You won't need yogurt, cow puss milk, soymilk, or anything else.

The fruit really dominates the sometimes-strong flavor of supplements. The texture of the smoothie makes them so easy to swallow you won't even know that they are in there. Allowing good things to flow into your body smoothly, without you having to ball your face up and choke it down.

Along with a basic mix of fruits, blend in one or more of the following:

- **Flax Seed*** (seeds blend up well in smoothies. They could contain minerals as well)
- **A liquid multi-vitamin***
- **A green superfood supplement***
- **A Fiber Powder***
- **A pro-biotic liquid*** (*good bacteria*)
- **Chlorophyll****
- **Liquid mineral supplement**** (*multi-vitamins often contain minerals as well*)
- **Maca Root powder**** (*a South American root excellent for the reproductive system*)
- **A red superfood supplement****(*this would contain Acia berries, Goji berries, etc.*)
- **Acia Berry Powder****
- **Spirulina****
- **Any other supplement you might be interested in**

Juice can be used in the smoothie, but try to avoid bottled juices, especially ones with processed sugar (*or HFCS—hell no!*), try to keep it all natural. Squeezing some real orange juice is so delicious but takes some time. Coconut water is excellent in smoothies if you want to try that. Plain water with the Agave or Maple syrup (or raw honey) turns out really sweet, I do it everyday.

For convenience you can use frozen fruit from a health food store, or use the fruit you get very affordably at the Eastern Market or Randazo's—clean it, then freeze it in small portions ready to drop in the blender with the other ingredients. Add a banana, or any piece of fresh fruit, add the supplements of your choice, and blend it up. It is fast and efficient. To make it even more hardy you can add oatmeal or tofu into your smoothie.

That is *real* fast food.

During a fast, a cleanse, or just on the day to day, smoothies are a great way to get a lot of nutrition quickly and its very tasty. Invest in a decent blender and get your drink on.

Teach the kids to make them and let that be a healthy but fun snack for them.

Make a smoothie and pour it into freezer trays and make popsicles out of them. Let our children conveniently enjoy real-fruit, chemical free snack that we all can feel good about! On the weekend, or on your birthday or whatever, throw some Rum in there with the real fruit and make a real Strawberry Daiquiri with real fruit and not "artificial strawberry flavors". You can even get your drink on naturally. Always stick with nature.

*These are items that I would strongly recommend you start to purchase from a health food store as you start your life transition. Staple items. As you learn more and begin to experiment, you might find other things that you like for you personally.

**These are things that came to me as I experimented more that I have enjoyed. Supplements can be expensive, especially buying them all at one time. Start off getting a few of the staple items and keep building from there.

A good multi-vitamin, a flax seed (like Forta-Flax), and a green powder is a solid start. On subsequent trips to the health food store you can add to your collection as you continue to grow.

E-mail any questions to: likeugiveadamn.com or post them on the website.

*(Smoothie recipes and demonstrations will be shown on the website: www.likeugiveadamn.com)*

# Chapter 11
# *Where should you Grocery shop?*

You cannot depend solely of the huge supermarket. I try to absolutely avoid if at all possible.

Remember farmer's markets are the best, and the less expensive place to get fresh produce. Other than that, try to stay in more conscious shopping venues. Many people in the Detroit area make their own products and we have to start moving more in that direction.

*Make sure you* plan on taking some extra time at these stores initially. You want to really read and investigate what you are going to be eating from now on. It is a learning process. It takes some time. You will start to learn which stores are good for which items along your transition to healthier food choices.

Here are a few of them.

*(FYI- all of these markets take the Bridge Card as well.)*

### *Whole Foods Market*
### *2 Locations*

**7350 Orchard Lake Road**          **1404 Walton Blvd**
**West Bloomfield, Michigan**        **Rochester Hills, Michigan**
**(8 a.m. until 10 p.m. 7 days)**    **(9 a.m. until 10 p.m. 7 days)**

**Overall:** Far away (for some) and it can be pretty expensive. They have a great selection and tasty "samples" throughout the store. Helps you to not shop hungry. It is a very clean and nice shopping atmosphere. All of your natural alternatives can be found there.

Don't go there with the idea that you are going to get EVERYTHING. Get the things that you can't find anywhere else ~ you will find that the smaller health food markets are cheaper more times than not. But, as the big company, they have EVERYTHING.

💣 The Bulk food items (couscous, tvp, etc.) The atmosphere. The samples. The hours are convenient. They have all the health products, so you can branch out slowly and educate yourself there.

*Natural Food Patch*
**221 W. Nine Mile Rd**
**(9 Mile between Woodward and Livernois)**
**Ferndale, Michigan**
**9 a.m. until 7 p.m. Monday thru Thursday**
**9 a.m. until 8 p.m. Friday and Saturday**
**10 a.m. until 6 p.m. Sunday**

    **Overall:** Small store, it has a really nice shopping atmosphere, very personable, pleasant people. They have way more than it appears they do. Mainly because we are used to huge "super" markets. There is not a lot of fresh produce, but it is all organic and reasonably priced. They do not sell any meat or fish.

💣 They have all of kinds teas. Soaps, detergents, cleaners, vitamins, healthy snacks, cleanses, and more. All the local healthy people shop at NFP, you can learn a lot by conversing with them. They have all the good snack and chip options.

*The Natural Food Patch in Ferndale*

## *Goodwell's Market*
**W. Willis at Cass Avenue**

**Overall:** Goodwell is a small, intimate market located on Cass and Willis. They have a great selection of healthy, light and delicious meals. They have the popular "pocket sandwich". Vegan desserts. Nice selection of organic produce. Fresh juices. It is a blessing to have it in the heart of the city. Helping to fill the void that the Co-op left.

💣 The soups are always the bomb! They have a really good selection of nuts. Priced very well. They have "a good selection of produce and healthy products. Goodwell's really has a family feel and it is a pleasure to spend finance with your own.

## *Sprout House Natural Food Market*
**15233 Kercheval Ave**
**Grosse Pte Park, MI 48230**
**(313) 331-3200**

**Overall:** Another small market with a nice selection of cooked health food choices, and a place where you can get stock up on some healthy grocery items. People living in that area have a good option of some quick healthy food and goods.

## *Trader Joe's*
**2 Locations: 11 Mile and Woodward.**
**14 Mile and N'Western Hwy.**

Trader Joes is a great shopping atmosphere and they have really good prices. They have a lot of healthy little snack type of foods. Frozen stuff that have better quality than the Market. They have some fresh produce, but not a whole lot. Tofurkey, Tempeh, Tofu, Hummus, salsa and stuff like that is priced well there and they have more health minded snacks for good prices.

💣 The snack type of stuff is really good here. Nice wine selection. 3 buck chuck! The water is priced well there. Plenty of better quality boxed and packaged stuff for transition.

## *Avalon Bakery*
**Cass & Willis**
**Detroit, MI**

**Overall:** Right next door to Goodwell's. This is a fun bakery that only uses the finest ingredients. A really cool atmosphere, they have fresh baked breads, desserts, and food available. Also fresh ground coffees, teas, jams, and butters. Conscious customers and a warm, cozy environment—plus Wifi.

🍓 The buns are so good! Put your veggie burger on that! They have sandwiches and salads as well. The bread and desserts are high quality, baked on site—and delicious.

## *Lovin' Goodies**
**Chef Mary B**
**248-779-7000**
**info@lovingoodies.com**
**West Bloomfield, MI 48325**

**Overall:** Lovin' Goodies provides organizations and individuals with an Eco Friendly guide to Gourmet Organic Raw Food, Health, Fashion and Beauty.
🍓 They provide classes, as well as sell affordable products and equipment that will help support your switch to a more health conscious lifestyle.

## *the Vegetarian express (a vegan food line)**
**Connie Vail & Laurie Snyman**
**(734) 355-3593**
**www.thevegetarianexpress.com**
**www.vegetarianseasonings.com**

**Overall:** Pre-packaged vegan foods and spices that are quick and easy to make! Order direct from their website. You can get ALL kinds fresh spices and mixes, and everything is vegan! Even a **vegan ranch dressing**, gravy, pancake mixes, and more.
🍓 Recipes are included as well. TVE boasts having: No Artificial Anything! No Hydrogenated Fats! No refined sugars!

## *Pure Food 2 U**
**(248) 549-5242**
**www.purefood2u.com**

**Overall:** Pure food 2 U delivers organic, freshly prepared authentic family meals to your home! They have a wide variety of choices, including weekly specials, and the prices are very reasonable. Especially considering the time it saves you.
🍓 PF2U offers it all: vegan, gluten free, raw, vegetarian, and natural meat meal options for breakfast, lunch, dinner and desert. Everything is made from scratch. Goodbye drive thru synthetic food. Hello real meals. Delivered!

---

*\*These are some really good, local resources that can really help make a lifestyle transition more feasible. Conveniently order food, products, and materials that are 100% made with health in mind. This is another way around the commercial grocery store.*

# Chapter 12
# *Stay Out of the Drive Thru!!!*

### *Eating Out*

I know that the pace of life demands that you eat out sometimes, make better choices about where you are going to eat.

One thing is obvious…stay OUT of the Drive Thru!!! That should not even be an option anymore.

Expand your mind. You are what you eat. You don't want to be the same old thing all the time!

Don't get locked into eating in too much of a pattern. When you are going out to eat, a good way to branch out is trying food from different cultures. American food consists of cheeseburger & lies with a Coke. Junk.

Step outside of this culture; take time to discover other types of cuisine. Go to a Japanese, Lebanese, or Thai restaurant for something different. It is always nice to discover new foods and dishes. Learn different cultures of food.

Sushi isn't ALL raw fish!! Grow up! We have to change our attitudes about new things. Adults are worse than children looking at something claiming you don't like it because of the way it looks or because it is new to you. It kills me how grown people are so closed minded. Need that cleanse!

People frown at my food ALL the time. But are you planning to do the "chicken wing and spaghetti" thing for your ENTIRE LIFE though? Live a little!

Indian and Ethiopian restaurants usually have lunch buffets, which is a good way to get a feel for their whole approach to food—try a little of everything. Mediterranean food is always good and freshly prepared. A lot of those dishes are light, healthy, and they have plenty of vegetarian options.

The **OM Café** on Woodward is one you must try. **Pita Cafe** in Southfield is almost guaranteed to become one of your favorites. Sala Thai (the eastern market one) is a really good one too, with a sushi bar inside as well. All of them have a different ambience ~ experience new things for a change.

Here is a list of some of the local places that you might want to check out:

(*If you want to recommend a place to everyone—please do so on our website:* Likeugiveadamn.com)

# Chapter 13
# List of Local Restaurants
## (A Few Good Places)

### Aladdin Sweets and Café (Indian Cuisine)
**11945 Conant St**
**Hamtramck, Michigan**
**11 a.m. to 11 p.m. Monday thru Thursday**
**11 a.m. to 1 a.m. Friday and Saturday**

Stays open until 1 on the weekend. Giving you a healthier alternative even at late hours. Very reasonably priced, and an authentic Bangladesh (Indian) cuisine. They are open for lunch buffet's as well. They also have a selection of desserts. The Detroit Zen Center is also in Hamtramck. There is a vegan and raw food cafe inside.

### Sala Thai
**Russell St.**
**Detroit, Michigan**
**11 a.m. to 10 p.m. Monday thru Saturday**

An old firehouse, it is a nice atmosphere with good Thai food. Light dishes and good service. Everyone I know who likes Thai goes here!
The Russell St one, in the Eastern market area taste better than the other locations for some reason. Ambience?

### AJ's Music Cafe
**(Vegetarian Cuisine)**
**W. Nine Mile**
**Ferndale, Michigan**
**8 a.m. to 11.pm 7 days a week**

They have a full vegetarian and vegan menu with a lot of options. They also have fresh soups, a good vegan chilli, & cookies and desserts - some of which are vegan (meat and dairy free). And delicious! They have a great coffeehouse atmosphere. They make fresh juices and have a variety of teas and coffees to choose from. Sunday morning they have a "vegan brunch", with waffles or tofu scramble with sausage. Cool off beat place.

## *The Blue Nile (Ethiopian)*
### W. Nine Mile
### Ferndale, Michigan

They offer fresh Ethiopian dishes with a lot of greens and beans. Really light and fresh food on platters—they encourage you to eat with your hands and share in a traditional Ethiopian style dining experience. Offers a very unique atmosphere. Try something different for a change!!

*The Blue Nile in Ferndale—offering Traditional Ethiopian Cuisine.*

## *Taste of Ethiopia*
### 2 locations:

| **Russell Street in the Eastern Market** (*the new one*) | **Southfield Rd, just north of 12 mile** (*near Burlington Coat Factory*) |
|---|---|

They have a sign that brags how they use "no canned vegetables" and add "no MSG" and "no processed ingredients". It is a natural and nice dining experience. The way dining out is supposed to be. Served in traditional Ethiopian style on platters. It is family owned with excellent food and service. Again – a chance to expose your family to delicious, educational, and cultural dining experience.

It is a hidden treasure in Southfield. Open for lunch buffet in Eastern market 6 days. Support it! The food is *awesome*.

## Byblos Café
**(Cass and Palmer – WSU area)**
**Detroit, Michigan**
**9 a.m. – 9 p.m. Monday thru Saturday**
**11 a.m. – 6 p.m. Sunday**

This is a nice place with fresh Middle Eastern cuisine. Try a Schwarma or a Fallafel sandwich. They also have fresh Lentil soup daily. Raw juices. The Fallafel "burger" is a nice alternative to a "meat" burger, try it out; They have wireless net available also.

## Motown Kabob
**Woodward just south of Grand Blvd**
**10- 9pm  Monday thru  Wednesday**
**10-10pm Thursday thru Saturday**

Authentic Middle Eastern cuisine at it finest, right in the hood! A much better option than that dirty a#@ Popeyes, or that nasty White Castle that sit across the street from it. They have it all including a raw juice bar! Convenient hours and location. Take advantage!

**Harmonie Way** (218 Grand River) is right in Harmonie Park offering good Middle Eastern cuisine as well. Check them out.

## Golden Gate Café & Innate Healing Center
**Goldengate & Woodward**
*(just north of 7 mile road)*

Interesting atmosphere. Interesting menu and interesting people; you will love the vibe at the hippie friendly vegetarian café in the hood! Drum circles on every Wednesday. They have bonfires outside. They have added a greenhouse. This is a peaceful and unique place that EVERYONE in the Detroit area should experience!! I don't know why they aren't on the "best of…" lists in local publications, it definitely should be. Dr. Bob and the crew are warm and peaceful.

## *Pita Café*
**Greenfield & 10 Mile**
**Oak Park**

The PC has fantastic Mediterranean cuisine, raw juices, and quality food and services. One of my personal favorite restaurants in the Detroit area period! The food is really good. Try something different. Enjoy.

## *Inn Season*
**East 4th Street just east of Main**
**Royal Oak**

ALL vegetarian restaurant that is really nice. Small and intimate, they also have fresh juices. They have a variety of dishes, from burgers, to Stir Fry's, baked spaghetti – and vegan/vegetarian desserts. Yum.

## *Honest Johns*
**Selden & Cass**
(**veggie burger & hummus…until 2 am.*)

You got the late night munchies? Hanging out downtown? The kitchen is open until 2 a.m. everyday, John is cool for that alone!! With a very vegetarian friendly menu ~ including hummus, veggie pita, and veggie burgers, and a veggie patty melt; local brews and an old school juke box to boot. Free Wifi (they actually sell and serve 40 Ounces of Black Label! Where you gonna find that at a bar?!) They also have a cool breakfast and open early too for hangover mornings.!

## *Lucy & Ethel's*
**Bagley & Cass**
(**veggie burger open 24 hrs on weekends. Hummus too. But they are sold out a lot.*)

Hungry even much later at night? Forget Cutters…L & E is open 24 hours on weekends and serve both hummus and a veggie burger. Goth /Punk rockers hang out there too, but they are cool—hope they don't buy all the veggie burgers (they sell out a lot)!! Rock on. Free Wifi.

## *The Woodbridge Pub*
**Trumbell just north of Warren**

They have the best Black Bean Burger that you have ever had period! And an overall good menu with plenty of health friendly eating choices, they also proudly use local ingredients. Try the Black Bean Burger! They have a vegan soup fresh daily –and other daily specials, it's a really cool atmosphere.

## *What Crepe?*
**317 S. Washington Ave.**
**Royal Oak, MI 48067**
**(248) 629-9391**
**www.whatcrepe.com**

What Crepe is a small and cozy French inspired café in downtown Royal Oak. Crepes (thin pancakes) come fancily stuffed with a variety of fillings, either "sweet" or "salty" as a dessert, or as a meal. What Crepe? offers both vegetarian and 100% vegan options—so there is something for everyone. Enjoy a unique dining experience. They also support local farms. Seek to do business with conscious places in this very important 'green' era.

You should also try *Good Girls Go To Paris Crepes* on John R and Woodward, downtown Detroit! www.goodgirlsgotopariscrepes.com

## *The Red Pepper Deli*
**116 W. Main St.**
**Northville, MI 48167**
**(248) 773 7671**

The Red Pepper Deli is a family owned and operated raw food restaurant! They have regular sandwiches and salads, plus daily specials, hot vegan soups, deserts, wheat grass, and organic tea/coffee. The works!!

## *mind body & spirits*
**301 S. Main St.**
**Rochester, MI 48307**
**248-651-FOOD (3663)**
**www.mindbodyspirits.com**

Talk about green? This place is unreal. Not only do they use local and organic produce. The historic building was rebuilt using sustainable materials like re-used brick, bamboo, and cork. They use eco-friendly cleaners, solar power, and re-use rainwater for the on-site greenhouse. Pinch me.

## Chapter 14
# *Endangered Species*

This handbook speaks to you from my personal experiences. Real life. I want you to really consider some of the things in this text. Value your life.

***Nothing* taste good enough to die for.**

I have known people that have passed away from heart attacks. Two of my co-workers at my old firehouse died in 2006 of heart attacks, ages 40 and 46. Those are numbers that I am approaching. That seriously caught my attention.

Several people I know have had double and triple bypass surgeries to repair blocked arteries. That is a heart attack waiting to happen. Even some of my peers, only in their young and mid 30's, are already on blood pressure medication, EVERYDAY of their life!

That is serious. What the hell is going on around here? When are we going to make some changes? These are our temples!

This food thing in our community has become quite an epidemic. We have to educate ourselves and make changes in our lifestyle. RIGHT NOW! That is why I speak with such fury. I want you to care! (…give a damn)

That is the bottom line, you have to care enough to control what is going inside your body. Life is so valuable, such a blessing. Preserve it.

Let your motivation come from wanting to live a long, healthy life. You want to experience everything, and that takes time. Don't let eating and food be your only pleasure. Taste becomes relative. You can learn to like things, especially natural things.

Beer doesn't taste good at all, it's actually disgusting, but we quickly learned to like it. Even if it's just for what it does for us. Look at food the same way if you have to. Appreciate it for what it does.

I have seen the results of someone having a heart attack. I know it probably hurts like hell— I don't ever want to go through that. Especially if all I have to do to avoid it is EAT some different stuff! Hell…I can do that!

**\*Here are a few numbers that illustrate just how much difference you can make with lifestyle changes:**

• AVERAGE U.S. MAN'S RISK OF DEATH FROM HEART ATTACK: **50** PERCENT

That is the *average* man. In urban communities, where fried food, fast foods, and stress are *saturating* the area—it is safe to assume the number is quite a bit *higher than that*!

• RISK OF AVERAGE U.S. MAN WHO EATS NO MEAT: **15** PERCENT

That is a lot better odds. And it says something about the humans being natural herbivores.

• RISK OF AVERAGE U.S. MAN WHO EATS NO MEAT, DAIRY OR EGGS: **4 PERCENT**!

4%. There we go. I am rolling with that one! I have been vegan for 5 years now and I feel great. I still enjoy eating. I prepare a number of interesting dishes, soups, salads, and smoothies. I've learned which types of restaurants I can visit to get good food. What I really enjoy is the fact that I am NOT going to have to worry about high cholesterol, or much about a heart attack—EVER!

Sure…you can joke and say my food 'looks nasty' all you want. Have your chicken dude! The results feel absolutely great! I wouldn't trade it for the world.

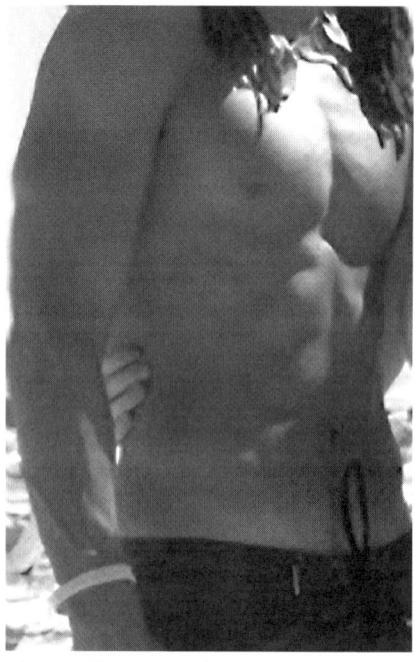

*And I would NOT trade bodies (OR BELLIES) with most of my peers either! Vegan does not equal skinny or weak!*

\**vegsource.com*

- **AMOUNT YOU REDUCE RISK OF HEART ATTACK IF YOU REDUCE CONSUMPTION OF MEAT, DAIRY, AND EGGS BY 50 PERCENT:** *45 PERCENT*

For those of you that can't give up meat totally, consider slowing down. Look into the family farms listed in this book. Maybe you'll get a little less quantity but the meat you get will come directly from a farm, so you know its not as processed and drugged. Stay away from that grocery store meat, and the poison fast food stuff. That would be a good place for you to start to change.

- **AMOUNT YOU REDUCE RISK IF YOU ELIMINATE MEAT, DAIRY AND EGGS FROM YOUR DIET:** *90 PERCENT!*

*The numbers say it all. I didn't make this up. Research it yourself.**

- **AVERAGE CHOLESTEROL LEVEL OF PEOPLE EATING MEAT-CENTERED-DIET:** 210 MG/DL.

Again, that is the *national* average. In the urban community you can probably set that number *higher*.

**Chance of dying from heart disease if you are male and your blood cholesterol level is 210 mg/dl:** *greater than 50 percent.*

So by *eliminating* meat, eggs, & dairy from your diet, you cut the risk of you having a heart attack by 90%!! Cholesterol (a.k.a. the animal's revenge) will becomes a total non-issue. Shock your 'doctor' with that ~ and flush the cholesterol and pressure pills! Animal products are **THE ONLY** source of cholesterol.

The incidence of high blood pressure is generally greater among meat-eaters than among vegetarians. Cancer of the breast, colon and prostate are most common among people on a high-meat, high-fat, low-fiber diet.

The journal of the National Cancer Society reports (via CNN) that animal fats, such as **red meat, cheese, ice cream, and butter greatly increase the risk of breast cancer in women.**

That is compelling enough evidence for me. If I know the stuff is no good for me, why not find other things to eat? This way I feel great and I know that I am healthy. Someone dies of a heart attack every 45 seconds in this country. I am NOT going to be in that number—the confidence to be able to say that, and know it, is absolutely priceless.

Re-examine your own life and think about exploring healthier ways for you and your family. I am here to support you.

Most of the products that are recommended in the "…Try this" section contain absolutely NO CHOLESTEROL! Substitute products with high cholesterol, for ones with ZERO cholesterol. That section (and shopping in the proper venues) is an excellent place to start the path towards a healthier life.

*vegsource.com

All you have to do is be open and willing to learn new things. Just examining these few numbers, you see it is time for a change. Don't take it from me.

Just how bad has health become in this country? Take a look at some of the numbers. It is staggering. Especially to think that it is only going to get worse.

- 72% of all Men in the U.S. are overweight *

- 62% of all Women in the U.S. are overweight *

- Over 9 Million Children are *Seriously* overweight. *

**This Year Alone:**

- 1.3 Million People will be diagnosed with Cancer *

- Over 1 million people will develop Diabetes this year *

- Over 975,000 will Die of Blood Vessel and Heart Disease *

- Over 550,000 will Die of Cancer (Treatment)! *

- Over 280,000 people will die from Obesity *

Look into it for yourself and you will see.
(Links are on the website likugiveadamn.com)

*Great American the Whole Food Farmacy: License to Kill*
*(google it)*

# Chapter 15
# *Reverse Evolution: From the Farm to the Pharmacy*

It is really very scary how fast paced we have become as a nation. Fast food, fast everything nation. (You are what you eat!) The younger generations coming up are losing touch with traditional medicines. There is a pharmacy on every corner these days.

Remember the days when grandma gave you a tablespoon of castor oil ~ for everything? Granny had all kinds of 'southern remedies' for even the oddest injuries—in the days before you ran to the emergency room for everything.

Those days have all but died. The grandmothers are much younger and of the microwave/cell phone generation. They are buying Hostess cakes, and using instant Oatmeal ~ instead of making biscuits from scratch, and slow boiling Oats the way they used to.

You can take this time to reverse that process in your own household.

Begin to think of more natural ways of healing your family. This culture has become too used to running out and "taking something" for any symptom that we are having. Don't flood your system with those chemical drugs.

When your child is sick, DO NOT immediately think to get "children's Tylenol" or any type of drugs. When you have a headache, I know it is uncomfortable, but you should not be quick to run out and grab some type of chemical drug for it.

Be old fashioned when it comes to your body.

Remember water and rest are the best medicines. Be still and let the body repair itself.

Drink herbal teas as medicine. There are hundreds of teas for numerous purposes. Use fresh lemon, fresh garlic, fresh onion, cayenne pepper—things that you probably have in your home already that are absolutely medicinal AND totally safe! There is no list of side effects with natural cures.

There are so many essential oils (eucalyptus, lavender, tea tree, etc.) and herbs that have been used for thousands of years as medicines by every culture. In fact, that is what the synthetic drugs attempt to emulate. Where do you think they get the ideas? There is nothing new in this universe. There is something in nature that

does exactly what everything in that pharmacy does.
*Except kill you.*

## *The Drug Game*

The FDA has made it "illegal" to claim that a natural remedy can effectively treat any dis-ease. In conjunction with that, they now categorize nearly everything as an official disease.

A child that is a little hyperactive (high on fructose corn syrup)—*now* has **ADD**. A person that is eating wrong and grossly overweight (eating hydrogenated oils)—*now* has **obesity disorder**. Once your symptoms are declared a disease, they are basically forced to prescribe drugs to you for treatment. The phony law says that ONLY a drug can effectively treat a disease.

That is the school of thought that your doctor is trained under. You have to remember that. That guy in a white lab coat is not God! Most of them are not fond of, or trained in herbal remedies or natural cures. They study MEDICINE not NUTRITION.

They have been trained by the same country that feeds you stuff to make you sick.

The US Medical system aims to steer people, just like they do the cattle, into using their harmful laboratory chemicals. Sending people flocking to the local neighborhood pharmacies, to take one of their drugs. It is THE largest industry in this country.

The goal in America (El Moroc) is not in educating people of the natural things that God (the sun) produces and that will keep us healthy. There is no money to be made in disease prevention, or disease cure. The money is in disease treatment!

These greedy drug companies and government agencies want to keep people taking their harmful laboratory drugs.

You have to harness the power within your self, and in nature to become a healer for your family. Keep yourself balanced.

Do not become a Guinea Pig for hospital experiments. These are numbers you don't want to be a part of:

- **250,000** PEOPLE WILL DIE THIS YEAR DUE TO HOSPITAL MISTAKES

- **12,000** DEATHS FROM UNNECESSARY SURGERIES IN HOSPITALS.

- **7,000** PEOPLE WILL DIE FROM MEDICATION ERRORS

- **20,000** people will die from other hospital errors.

- **80,000** People will die due to Nosocomial infections in hospitals.

- **106,000** People will die from Adverse Effects from (new) Prescription Medications.

## *The Herb is the Word*

*The Good Health Store* on Mack has a nice herb selection. They have books that can help you determine which herbs you may need to utilize most.

To start off myself, I began to randomly pick a couple different herbs each weekend at the Market to build a little collection. A natural medicine cabinet if you will. I would literally google them when I got home and research what they had been used for traditionally.

I found many interesting herbs, with long histories. White Willow Bark was one of the random herbs that I picked. I found an interesting story about the herb:

**White willow bark is the original aspirin. The medicinal use of willow bark dates back to the Greek physician Hippocrates (400 B.C.), (you know when they write that, it really comes from Hotep and the Egyptians of course!!) who advised his patients to chew on willow bark to reduce fever and inflammation. It has been used through the centuries in China and Europe. It became really popular in the 1800's-so popular that it caught the interest of the German company Bayer. Bayer found and created a synthetic derivative called acetyl-salicylic acid (aspirin) and mass-produced it.**

How interesting is that? Now days, when I offer a capsule of *White Willow Bark*, with explanation, to someone—they look at it with an uneasy frown. "Un-uh...I don't know about that stuff. I need some real medicine"

You see how backwards we have been trained to think today? The plant that has been growing for centuries out of the earth, we look at as "that funny stuff".

But a pill that was produced in a laboratory—which will kill you if you take 20 of them by the way—that is the "real" medicine??? WTF?

We are so used to looking at and taking the synthetic man made products (and food) that we ignore the natural herbs that have been around for literally thousands of years! That is a Nature made medicine! All real medicines lie in nature.

Of course they do not teach us that in schools. A school's job is to make cattle. Doctors included, they are trained in institutions that promote chemicals over nature. They have Coke machines all over the campus! That is the place where people are taught about natural health? NO!

Sadly, we have to take it upon ourselves to discover real medicine. You can start by staying with what you do know. Herbal teas. Lemon, Garlic, Onion, Cayenne - start to think of those things in terms of medicine and branch out from there.

Utilize some of these venues where people are experienced in herbal medicines. Talk to people, get your google on, and start to explore some more nature based ways of maintaining your temple.

# Chapter 16
# *Herb-ology*

The world of herbs is absolutely fascinating. It shows some indication of the vast intelligence of ancient civilizations had of this land that we are now destroying.

It also clearly illustrates that all we need to maintain ourselves lies within nature. The science of nature is simple, yet divine. The Creator has provided us with all that we need indeed.

Herbs that grow in specific areas usually have adjusted to that area or environment. These herbs are generally good for dis-eases of that specific area. For example, herbs that grow in mountains are good for the lungs, resistance to cold, and other things dealing with that type of environment.

Herbs that grow in water aid in resistance to circulatory illness, blood system of organs, and other circulatory functions of the body. Herbs that grow in the dessert-like areas help to stabilize body temperature, keep moisture in the skin, and protect you from ultra-violet rays. Amazing!

That is just a tiny idea of how nature provides us with everything that we need, without relying on man-made imitations of the divine.

Here is a list of just a few disorders and the herbs that have been used to treat them for many centuries. A complete listing would be beyond this publication. But I encourage you to check out some books of herbs ~ the history and the many present-day uses.

## *Anemia*
**Agrimony • Century • Comfrey • Dandelion (yes that dandelion) • Fenugreek Red Clover • Yellow Dock**

## *Blood Circulation (increasing)*
**Cayenne • Gentian • Goldenseal • Holy Thistle • Hyssop • Witch Hazel**

## *Bowel*
## *(Digestive Problem, Constipation)*
**Catnip • Comfrey • Dandelion • Fenugreek • Goldenseal •Magnolia • Marshmallow • Tansy • Witch Hazel**

## *Bronchitis*
Chickweed • Coltsfoot • Elecampane • Ginger • Goldenseal • Mullein • Pleurisy • Saw Palmetto • Skunk Cabbage • Slippery Elm

## *Colds/Flu/Fever*
Bayberry • Cat's Claw • Chickweed • Cloves • Elecampane • Horehound • Mullein • Pleurisy • White Pine Bark

## *Coughs*
Black Cohosh • Coltsfoot • Comfrey • Flaxseed • Ginseng • Goldenseal • Horehound • Hyssop • Lungwort • Myrrh • Origanum • Pleurisy • Red Sage

## *Eczema*
Balomy • Bloodroot • Calendula • Chickweed • Dandelion • Goldenseal •Nettle • Plantain • Primrose • Yellow Dock

## *Fever*
Angelica • Bitterroot • Borage • Buckbean • Calamus • Catnip • Cat's Claw • Cayenne • Cinchona • Cleavers • Dandelion • Echinacea • Feverfew • Hyssop • Indian Hemp • Lily of the Valley • Lobelia • Mandrake • Nettle • Sumac Berries • Tansy • Thyme • Valerian • Vervian • Wahoo • Willow • Wintergreen • Yarrow

## *Hemorrhoids*
Aloes • Bittersweet • Burdock • Goldenseal • Myrrh • Nettle • Sheppard's Purse • White Oak Bark • Uva Ursa

## *Pneumonia*
Black Cohosh • Bloodroot • Coltsfoot • Comfrey • Elecampane • Horehound • Marshmallow • Peruvian Bark • Red Sage • Skunk Cabbage • Spikenard • Vervain • Wild Cherry • Willow

## *Thyroids*
Cayenne • Irish Moss • Kelp • Pau D'Arco • Parsley

Do your research for the exact usages and dosage. Make sure you understand and are very aware that there are many natural herbal alternatives for EVERY health disorder that you can think of.

These are the type of things that you want to begin to learn about. Get a book. Shop at farmer's markets and stores that carry some of these herbs, and begin to form a knowledge base. Teach your children.

*Herbal teas* are available at health stores. The box would have the origin, history, and dosage recommendations for that particular herb. Use that as medicine.

If, for instance, you are experiencing problems with your thyroid, having 2 or 3 cups of Pau D'arco tea daily could certainly help your body regulate the situation.

The worse case is you just enjoy a few good cups of herbal tea. It is NOT going to harm you. But throughout the history of the world, it has been known to help with thyroid situations. Why not try it? Even in addition to whatever the doctor may have prescribed?

Get your google on! Utilize the medicines that our ancestors used before the CVS, the Rite Aid, and the drugs were option #1. That is nature's (God's) medicine. Pick that over man made stuff any day!

You can brew herbal teas—add lemons, ginger, honey, and/or oranges, whatever you prefer. Creating a refreshing, yet healthy iced tea to enjoy. That is a far cry from a can of sugar filled iced tea! Be creatively conscious ~ share any ideas with your friends and family! I will be glad to post them on the website.

The mentality has to return to the old school way of thinking. Make and grow medicine at home, don't take these new, commercial laboratory drugs.

I do understand that this is a lot. Life is hectic, and it is hard to take time to locate and gather all of the information you need. Here are some excellent local resources that you can turn to who are skilled in the herb healing area and will be glad to assist you.

## *Local Detroit Area Herbal Resources:*
### *Dr. Isis*

Dr. Isis is a Detroit Area natural health practitioner who has been helping people discover natural remedies for many years. She is a skilled healer and works in Detroit's worst neighborhoods bringing wisdom to her people. She has a masterful understanding of herbs. She makes her own products, including a Miracle 8 cream, which is useful for a variety of ailments. Even serious ones!

I really appreciate the knowledge and direction that the Queen blessed me with! I encourage you to set up a consultation with her and benefit from her ancestral wisdom. Her flyers hang in 'hood' party stores, often times over the vulgar malt liquor ads. She is a blessing to the Detroit community.

She is available at 313.213.2166 (Tell her Ra-One sent you)

### *Love Earth Herbal Teas*

The Love Earth Herbal is a great herbal tea resource that you to take advantage of. Upon your request, they will hand make organic teas, using fresh herbs that are specific to whatever condition you may need. The teas are available in 7, 14, or 21-day supplies and are guaranteed fresh. Made with nothing but loving and healing energy.

Last year when my mother was diagnosed with slight pneumonia in the lungs, she enjoyed and benefited from the homemade herbal, organic tea that Love Earth provided. You will appreciate and taste the love in the products as well! Order some organic tea for anyone who you think may benefit from some of nature's (God's) original medicine! They accept money order, or Paypal.

Available at: love.earth.herbal@gmail.com

*Eastern Market in summer time, various fresh herbs for the low-low. You can grow them on your window seal. Start teaching your children that you can grow live medicine instead of taking pills! That is valuable.*

# Chapter 17
# Alternative Medicine

Chemical drugs DO NOT treat the actual source of the problem. So-called medicines (drugs) treat the symptoms, not the source!

It would be like a car that has an electrical problem that keeps causing the taillight to burn out. Taking a drug for your symptom is like going to get another type of taillight. It will temporarily alleviate the symptom (having no lights), but the source of the issue, the electrical problem, is not resolved or addressed.

Therefore more serious problems are bound to occur in the future.

That is the Western approach to medicine. When more problems arise, they just simply prescribe more powerful drugs (cover ups). Doctors get paid to prescribe medicines. The new stuff even gets cool, celebrity endorsements these days! (With that long list of side effects at the end.) It is commerce. They are promoting brand new drugs.

The more natural approach to medicine is to simply maintain the body. Keeping all channels open and letting the body flow properly and balance itself as it was intended to do. Using herbs, diet, vibration, meditation, and the spirit to achieve balance and harmony within the body. That is the innate, natural approach to health.

Many gems, stones, crystals, (and herbs) date back to the earliest civilizations as being used medicinally. Everything that you need has been here long before you. There is no such thing as a new medicine ~ only new drugs.

Things like: Colon Hydrotherapy, Acupuncture, Chiropractors, Massage Therapy, and Yoga represent that more natural approach to maintaining the temple (body).

### Acupuncture

Acupuncture is one of the oldest healing practices in the world. It aims to restore and maintain health through the stimulation of specific points on the body. The practice aims to achieve an internal balance and let the body's vital energy flow freely along their pathways, known as meridians. Something you may consider looking into as opposed to brand new chemicals ~ which have no track record at all. Set up a consultation with an Acupuncturist to learn more about how a treatment can benefit you personally.

## *Chiropractic Healing*

The Chiropractic approach to medicine involves aligning, and restoring structural integrity to the spine. Throughout the course of our lives the spine, where all nerve ending stem from, "loses some of its structural integrity. Chiropractors aim to restore the proper alignment through a series of 'adjustments' ~ aiming at free flowing energy throughout the body. It works by allowing the body to heal, and alleviating pain without the use of medicines or surgery.

The chief complaint I hear from people is that they want you to get adjusted as often as possible. Several times a week in the beginning, and it can be hard given people's daily schedules. It feels absolutely great to have your back and neck methodically cracked. Try to find an office in close proximity.

## *Massage Therapy*

Massage therapy is the systematized manipulation of soft tissues for the purpose of normalizing them. The massage therapist uses a variety of physical methods including applying fixed or movable pressure, holding, or causing movement to the body. The basic goal of massage therapy is to help the body heal itself and increase health.

Touch conveys a sense of caring, an important component in healing. Massage improves circulation, which increases the blood flow, bringing fresh oxygen to the body tissues. This can assist the elimination of waste products, enhance self-esteem, while boosting circulatory and immune systems to benefit blood pressure, circulation, muscle tone, digestion, and skin tone.

## *Yoga*

Yoga is an ancient art form aimed to unite the body, mind, and spirit ~ finding harmony between them all. When people think of yoga, you may imagine having to stretch like a gymnast. You are never to old or tight to take up yoga and improve your flexibility.

By safely stretching the muscles, yoga releases the lactic acid that builds up with muscle use. It helps to alleviate muscle stiffness, tension, pain and fatigue.

Many yoga poses (called asanas) are accompanied by breathing and/or meditation techniques—throughout history it is known to have many positive effects on the body and mind. There are too many to list, among them: Increase circulation, pain decreases, balance improvement, respiratory efficiency increases, weight normalizes, hostility decreases, and many more. It is proven that yoga can aid in glucose, sodium, and total cholesterol decreases as well.

## *Breathing*

Breathing is an essential body function that we take for granted. Some ancient cultures reasoned that we live a certain number of breaths in a lifetime, and time was no factor.

You can practice deep, slow breathing anytime. Breathing, like fasting is another 'no purchase necessary' form of detoxification.

It is said we breathe over 100,000,000 breaths in our lifetime. The unclean air we breath, along with shallow breathing can help cause toxicity in the lower portion of the lungs. That can contribute to people feeling sluggish and unmotivated. Another area we can detoxify through deep breathing techniques.

Close your eyes, sit upright and comfortable, and draw deep slow breaths through your nose. In your mind see and feel the cool air going deep into your lungs. Blow out any toxins or stagnant energy stored deep inside. For a pick-me-up or just to exercise the lungs, repeat that process 21 times. Many eastern philosophy books outline several different breathing exercises. It is a good idea to spend some time controlled breathing everyday.

## *Movement*

Movement is life. You notice that all of these practices work towards your body healing itself. Improving circulation helps the temple detoxify and alleviate waste on its own. Disease does not have a chance to set in a well circulating, moving system.

It is true that a flowing body of water is an alive electric current. It attracts life. It produces new life and energy. While a stagnant body of water is dying, it attracts dis-ease and mosquitoes. It becomes impure. Your body is over 70% water, and without question you want to keep your fluids moving. That will ensure you have the energy to enjoy the great gift of life!

Talk to a friend or family member about attending a beginner's yoga class. Consider going to get a cleanse, or getting a massage once a month or so. As you start to discover things on your own, you will find that these things are absolutely medicinal. Restore your youth and health using safe, natural practices.

Peace and good health to you always. Good luck in your personal journeys. I hope that this has helped you along your path. Thank you for reading.

> **Come on in and treat your soul with healthy eating!**
>
> 1.) Experience a new beginning to healthy eating!
>
> 2.) No MSG!
>
> 3.) No saturated fat!
>
> 4.) No frozen food nor canned food!
>
> 5.) For those who are health conscious, "TASTE OF ETHIOPIA" is the answer

*The window of the TASTE OF ETHIOPIA ~ the new face of soulfood.*

## Chapter 18

# *Outro*

> "...Ever read the label on food packages? They think so little of your intelligence they list all the stuff they put in food to kill you! You see twelve words you cant pronounce and you eat it anyway. All them chemicals, preservatives, sugar, and poisons they add to food that ain't nutrition, that's behavior modification! America is the number one hoarder of money, land, natural resources, and food. We eat more food more often than any other nation, and then carry it around inside for seven weeks, seven months, seven years, seventy years. That's why you all stink. Your armpits, your bad breath, they're tellin' you that you stink from what you eat! From what's rottin' inside of you…"

—*Dick Gregory March 1, 1981*
*Bristol, Rhode Island*
*Introduction from:*
*Survival Into The 21st Century*
*Planetary Healers Manual*

Mr. Gregory said that in 1981, nearly 30 years ago—and not much has changed. Except the ingredients list 20 words you can't pronounce now instead of just twelve. Not only that, but in this day and (information) age the Internet gives us all a tool to learn exactly what those things are AND what they do to us.

But even that isn't enough to make a difference. People are STILL eating the sh*t anyway.

I actually HEAR people talking lightly, nearly joking about the "steroids in that chicken" making kids grow up so fast these days! So we clearly KNOW what is happening to us on some level. But yet we still order 'strips and fries', or nuggets for OUR own children? What the hell is going on?

If you know it ain't right—**GET OFF OF THE DAMN CHICKEN ALREADY!!!**

We don't have the wherewithal to control what is going in our temples and I don't understand it. Maybe we don't understand the blessing that the body truly is; or just don't appreciate the blessing of life!

The news fills our heads with so much negativity. So much violence and sorrow is around us that on some level subconsciously we may want to kill ourselves. Our mentality is hopeless, just like the chickens born and raised in indoor cages, waiting to be slaughtered in mass.

They don't say you are what you eat for nothing.

We trap ourselves. We seem firmly convinced that killing ourselves is perfectly cool—as long as it tastes good!

**America is now serving artificially flavored suicide. Over billions served.**

Hopefully this and my forthcoming books will help to awaken people. Please use this information to spark some changes in your lifestyle. I watch the people I love, my family and friends, eating this stuff that is slowly killing them and it hurts me to the core.

I see my uncles and elders taking prescribed chemicals every single day—and it bothers me to no end.

**This is *your* body.** Life is the greatest blessing that you can have, when are we finally going to wake up? We have to take control over what we allow in our bodies. Take back control of our minds! I offer this in hopes that people love themselves enough to care. If you want to change and I will do my best to connect you with the resources that will help show you how.

If we can learn to preserve our self, we can save the earth. We need to restore our natural thought process. Restore humanity. It starts when we begin to take care of our own temples.

> **I speak the truth and it hurts, so people call me a radical. This is a revolution. We want to improve the lives of the people. There is no room for compromise.**
>
> —*Antoine Izmery*

# Chapter 19
## *The Love Movement*

People today will go out of their way to explain in detail to you the things which they absolutely CANNOT STAND! We focus way too much energy on things that we don't like, and can't change.

It's nothing to hear someone describing the way they feel about something say, "I hate that!"

It's probably best not to use the word 'hate' at all. We say that word for even the most trivial things. Try to point it out to people that you speak with.

My ears have become very sensitive to it. The word itself carries such an ugly connotation with it. It is an extremely strong energy. You can almost feel the vibration of the word.

Do you really "hate" anything? Don't default to saying that when you happen to dislike something.

Say that you 'don't really care for it'. Or that it is 'not one of your favorite things.'

Utilize the vocabulary. There are many more words you can use to express yourself.

We really need to check ourselves because out of habit, without noticing, people will say the word "hate" more times throughout the day than we say the word "love". Lots more.

That is a horrible imbalance! Sickness and dis-ease come from imbalance of energy, even in the word that we use. We have the power to speak things into existence (spell).

You don't want such harsh (negative) energy constantly coming from your being! That is not the vibration you want coming towards you either.

Understand that you ARE A CREATOR!! Speak positive vibrations into existence always. That will in turn bring positive, healthy energy to you!

"*...now don't you understand man Universal Law? What you put out comes back to you star...*"

—*Lauryn Hill*

Again, constant complaining and negative attitudes are clear signs of discord inside the body. Clean it out. Fussing about something will never make anything better. Why bother?

A crucial step in changing your overall health is simply choosing to live your life optimistically. Lift your own spirits. You have to want to feel good. Stop constantly talking about what is bothering you!

Big picture it! Appreciate life first. Open your eyes each morning like it is just the gift you have always wanted! (And it will be.)

Spend your energy detailing things that you actually do like. And love. Share those things with everyone. The things that make you YOU! That is the energy the universe needs from your being.

Correct your family and friends when they are ranting about what they supposedly 'hate'. Start pointing this out to them. (Buy them a copy of this book!)

Focusing on things that you love will make your days much easier. That alone will keep your blood pressure lower and have you healthier.

As you begin your lifestyle transition remember to stay positive and watch how quickly you begin to attract positive vibes!

Don't dwell on how hard it is to give up certain things initially, but instead focus on how much you will love the way you feel after your body is clean and re-energized.

Try new foods and venues with a positive mind. Taste things inquisitively, without a frown on your face. Expect to love it! Realizing that it is just something you might not have been exposed to and therefore a bit unusual. Different does not mean nasty!

Appreciate it, as it is simply a part of your growth process. Treat it as an opportunity for you to learn new things and have new experiences in life.

*For that alone, you have to love it!*

*Hotep. Peace and love to you all.*

# Chapter 20
# Glossary of Terms

## ~Vegetarian~
Vegetarians do not eat animal flesh. Most vegetarians however do continue eat animal by products (i.e. milk, cheese, eggs, etc).

## ~Vegan~
(Pronounced vee-gun) A Vegan diet is one that does not include animal flesh OR any animal products at all. It is often the next step after a vegetarian diet as the body and mind start to change.

## ~Raw Foodist~
Anyone who eats 60% or more of their food raw or live is by definition considered a "rawist" or "rawfoodist." The next step to a Vegan diet is often going on a "raw" diet. Consisting of mainly raw fruits and vegetables, and nuts. Some people on raw diets include raw nuts and seeds many, however, do not.

Your body has a finite number of enzymes. Enzymes are what is used to break food down in your system. Raw, or living food (i.e. an apple) is alive and contains active enzymes. Thus saving your body from having to use its own. Therefore raw food essentially breaks itself down. Saving the bodies internal energy and preserving life force. After years of eating many people you know may have reflux, or gas, or heartburn, etc. All of those are results of a depleted digestive system.

**Fruitarian** would be the next step.

### (Grains)
## ~Couscous~
(Pronounced "koos-koos") is a staple of North African cooking, is now widely available in packaged form in most supermarkets. It is used just like rice is used in Asian cultures. Moroccan stews are most often served over couscous.

It is simple to prepare - usually you just add boiling water and let it sit. You can add exotic spices or sauces or leave it plain. It can be a salad base, a filling addition to soups, an accompaniment for meats and vegetables, and if sweetened, spiced and mixed with dried fruits, a dessert.

Try to use couscous as a replacement with a different flair to it. Stir Fry some vegetables and some tempeh—serve it over a bed of couscous! (nat. food patch, trader joes, etc)

## ~Quinoa~

(Pronounced keen-wah) is an ancient food that is not yet well known in North America. It has been cultivated in South American Andes since at least 3,000 B.C. and has been a staple food of millions of native inhabitants. The ancient Incas called quinoa the "mother grain" and revered it as sacred.

The quinoa seed is high in protein, calcium and iron, a relatively good source of vitamin E and several of the B vitamins. It contains an almost perfect balance of all eight essential amino acids needed for tissue development in humans. It is exceptionally high in lysine, cystine and methionine-amino acids typically low in other grains. It is a good complement for legumes, which are often low in methionine and cystine.

**The protein in quinoa is considered to be a complete protein due to the presence of all 8 essential amino acids**. Some types of wheat come close to matching quinoa's protein content, but grains such as barley, corn, and rice generally have less than half the protein of quinoa.

(Quinoa at Natural Food Patch (most health food stores) in spaghetti or macaroni noodle form. Or its available in bulk as an oatmeal type of grain.)

### (Meat Replacements)

## ~Seiten~

(Pronounced say-tahn) Seitan is derived from the protein portion of wheat. It stands in for meat in many recipes and works so well that a number of vegetarians avoid it because the texture is too "meaty."

Making seitan and gluten will open up a new horizon for you in the world of vegetarian cooking. It is terrific in stir-fries and paired with noodles in Asian-style dishes, yet also works well in traditional American fare like stew. Try substituting it for animal products in former favorite recipes or those of non-vegetarian friends and relatives. Then get your creative juices flowing and experiment when making seitan by varying the flavorings and cooking methods.

Try a Seiten Rueben from AJ's Café on 9 Mile. Get it with a Mango smoothie or a cup of their veggie chili in the Detroit weather. A can't miss - its delicious!!

## ~Tempeh~

(Pronounced Temp-pey) is a fermented food made by the controlled fermentation of cooked soybeans. It has been a favorite food and staple source of protein in Indonesia for several hundred years. Tempeh is now starting to gain popularity all over the world.

Vegetarians and vegans find the structure and protein content interesting. Tempeh has a firm texture and a nutty mushroom flavour. It can be used in many different ways. Normally it is sliced and fried until the surface is crisp and golden brown —or tempeh can be used as ingredient in soups, spreads, salads and sandwiches.

(Try the Om Café' has a Tempeh Burger. Also Inn Season in Royal Oak.)

I (used) to sauté Tempeh in soy butter and/or a little Olive Oil, fresh garlic, fresh onion, with lemons to squeeze over it. Cook it until golden brown in little strips. You can do that "chicken-like" strips in stir frys or just over couscous.

## ~ Tofu ~

(Pronounced Tow-foo) is made from soybeans, water and a coagulant, or curdling agent. It is high in protein and calcium and well known for its ability to absorb new flavors through spices and marinades. Due to its chameleon-like qualities and nutritional value, tofu, a staple of Asian cuisines for hundreds of years, has recently become popular in Western vegetarian cooking.

It has almost become synonymous with vegetarianism itself. When looking at Tofu there are two different kinds: silken or soft Tofu, and firm or regular Tofu. They would be used when different textures are needed. You could make for instance a Tofu scramble (like scrambled eggs) from a soft Tofu. And perhaps cut cubes of the firm Tofu into a Stir-fry to replace chicken.

(All Thai places will replace meat with Tofu in their dishes. Tofu Scramble is available at the Woodbridge Pub, and Golden Gate for Sunday brunch. Even the grocery store should have tofu. Tofu scrambled with fresh bell peppers, onions, and curry powder…is whassup.)

## ~ T.V.P ( Textured vegetable protein) ~

tvp is defatted soy flour, by product of making soy bean oil; It high in protein and low in fat. Can replace beef in a lot of recipes. Sloppy joes, tacos, burritos and chilli.

TVP in chili taste just like ground beef is in it. It replaces ground beef perfectly in ANY recipe that you can think of. Without a diseased animal being on your plate

## ~ Wheatgrass~

Refers to the young grass of the common wheat plant, Triticum aestivum, which is freshly juiced or dried into powder for animal and human consumption. Both forms provide chlorophyll, amino acids, minerals, vitamins, and enzymes. Claims about wheatgrass health benefits range from providing supplemental nutrition to having unique curative properties.

It is said that one shot of wheatgrass juice has the nutritional value of 5 pounds of leafy green vegetables. Many consider the juice from the plant a 'superfood'. It is not edible.

Most healthy juice/smoothie bars offer shots of wheatgrass. It should be taken on an empty stomach. It taste just like grass of course. (Like you'd picked a handful of grass and drank it.

The list of health benefits surrounding wheatgrass is quite impressive; there are of course skeptics to the many positive things regarding wheatgrass. They include: improves the digestive system, prevent diabetes, heart disease, cure constipation, detoxify heavy metals from the bloodstream, help make menopause more manageable, and promotes general well-being.

At health food stores you can find a whole section of green superfood powders that supplement green foods in your diet. They often include wheatgrass. It is available in frozen form at most health food stores, including the Natural Food Patch in Ferndale.

You can get a shot in the coffee shop in the Compuware building. Try it a couple of times a week. Chase it with an apple

## ~Steeping Tea~
Tea can be steeped for as little as a half a minute, or as long 20 minutes. For a mild cup of tea, steep from 1 to 3 minutes, for a stronger, more therapeutic/medicinal dosage, steep between 5 and 20 minutes.

After pouring the hot water over the tea bag, place a small saucer over the cup and let it steep.

## ~Spirulina~
(Pronounced Spear-a-leena) Is a friendly bacteria cultivated around the world, and is used as a human dietary supplement as well as a whole food and is available in tablet, flake, and powder form. It is a rich source of potassium and also contains calcium, chromium, copper, iron, magnesium, manganese, phosphorus, selenium, sodium, and zinc.

It is also a complete protein containing all essential amino acids. It can be added to smoothies or taken in tablet form as a dietary supplement.

# SOURCE LIST AND RECOMMENDED READINGS

**Prescription to Nutritional Health by Phyllis A. Bach, CNC**
This is a MUST-HAVE around the house. DRUG-FREE remedies, treatments and dietary suggestions for nearly EVERY health problem you can think of. Stop running to CVS and learning what herbs, minerals, and foods that can help heal you. This is a tool you will need to begin to do that.

**Survival into the 21st Century – Planetary Healers Manual– by Viktoras Kulvinskas, M.S.** (introduction by Dick Gregory)
This is a book from 1975 and it is amazing. Everything in it is still very valid today! It talks about some of the problems environmentally that excessive meat would cause that we see happening right now. The hippie's health book ~ Amazon it! Become one with the universe.

**African Holistic Health – Llaila O. Afrika**
A comprehensive book with loads of information about health and history. Dr Afrika also has a DVD series out with a lot of original medicine instructions.

**Nutricide – Llaila O. Afrika**
Dr. Afrika's latest work that illustrates how bad diet and food is destroying us and the earth. Also a DVD. Really heavy stuff.

**Choosing Life guidelines to avoiding extinction – Dr. Michael C. Frost Ph.D.**
A comprehensive book with a wealth of information on the Ancient Traditions of Tao— it has some great (and ancient) principles. Have an open mind and this book can really open your mind up!

**Natural Cures – Kevin Trudea**
I'm kind of sick of the infomercials and all that too. But this book really helped shift my thought process regarding what I was going to allow inside my body. Therefore, it helped change my life. It has valid information.

**Heal Thyself For Health and Longevity - Queen Afua**
A must have book that goes over fasting, healing, and healthy life transitions. It covers a great deal of information. The Queen inspires me and I know this work will help you in your expansion.

**Skinny Bitch – Rory Freedman & Kim Barnouin**
This is a hardcore, tough love type of book breaking down the food industry. It is full of very relevant information and it's talking in real talk. I love it. People have to get this message by any means necessary! There is a wealth of thoroughly backed up facts between cuss words. No BS!

# LINKS

**www.detroitagriculture.org**
'Grown in Detroit' this is an awesome program. They are taking vacant lots or your yard or porch and helping turn them into food producing areas. This is absolutely the type of thing we need support. They offer classes look online or see them at the market every Saturday to get involved.

**www.detroitevolution.com**
Offering yoga classes, raw food classes, catering and more—a great local resource.

**www.meatrix.com**
This is a really cute cartoon that describes the industry-farming nightmare. A must see for your family.

**www.soulveg.com**
A cool network of folks with "soul" that are still health conscious. Vegetarians, vegans, and raw foodist alike log on and share recipes and success stories. It is an excellent network to join for support in your time of transition.

**www.truthinlabelling.com**
Breaks down label lingo, and what some of the long words really refer to. It shows you just what to look out for. Manufacturers often try to hide their harmful ingredients with colorful words. "Natural flavors" can really mean as many as 30 chemicals.

**www.eatwild.com**
Links across the country for independent, humane farms that raise animals and produce naturally. You can go visit a farm in your area and see the difference.

**www.eatraw.com**
Nice website with organic and raw products available for your purchase. They offer bulk rates as well. Perhaps this is another alternative way of getting better quality goods than you can get at a grocer.

**www.chocolatedecadence.com**
CHOCOLATE!! Dairy free. Lactose free. Casein free. Gluten free. Vegan.

**www.nutrilicious.com**
A vegan, gluten free, lactose free, sugar free, cholesterol free bakery. Doughnuts and all! Now what's your excuse?

**www.vegan.meetup.com/99/**
A Vegan group in Michigan that meets throughout the year and has some cool events lined up. Get involved. Feel the support, learn a lot, and have some healthy fun!

**www.vegmichigan.org**
This is the largest vegetarian group in Michigan. Their website has a lot of information, including events that take place throughout Michigan. The group aims to educate people of the many health and environmental benefits of a plant-based diet. Another great resource!

**detroitblackfoodsecurity.org**
The Detroit Black Community Food Security Network is creating model urban agricultural projects that seek to build community self-reliance, and to change our consciousness about food.
This nonprofit organization is seeking to educate people about healthy eating, agriculture, co-operative shopping, and much more. Go to the website, visit their gardens and get involved. This is absolutely the way we need to think about controlling the food in our community going forward. The resources are definitely accessible.

**therunningstonesteppers.com**
This is a local area running group that trains and competes in local and national events. Now that you have decided to adopt a new lifestyle, how about picking up a new healthy hobby? Bring your spouse or friend and join the running group! They accommodate all levels of runners. Any shapes or sizes are very welcome. My big brother Mike Stone is a world class motivator!

# Source DVD's

For information regarding where to get these DVD's and lectures check the website or send an email to likeugiveadamn.com for information.

### Dr. Lailo Afrika (Many Titles)

Dr Afrika's DVD's are very informative and interesting things surrounding real nutrition (nutricide), astrology, and more. He has done quite a few DVD's. He also comes to Detroit to give lectures.

### Dr. Sebi – (Your Leaders Have Betrayed You, others.)

Dr. Sebi is an herbal doctor and healer, with quite an interesting story and DVD. He claimed to have a cure for Aids, the US Supreme court sued him about it, and he won! This one is a must see. He may some other titles as well. He has interesting theories about food and medicine.

### The Rave Diet (Eating)

A video about health and nutrition that offers among other things testimonies of people that had been cured of serious disease by simply adopting raw, and vegan diets. This DVD was really a major step in my personal growth. My cousin Calvin and my boy Hill-Harris showed it to me on the same day at Engine 1. I knew it was a sign.

   Not that it is the most entertaining video in the world, but it just put me over the top. I couldn't live the same anymore. I no longer had ignorance as an excuse. Once you know what the deal is, you have to decide if you are going to make changes, or ignore the obvious and eat your life away. Its really that simple.

   My allergies were harsh man! I could not breath at night at all in spring or the fall. As soon as I totally rid my body of meat and dairy, they were GONE. Immediately. That was no joke. So while I did love cheese, I had to decide if I love cheese more than breathing.

   My mind was made up.

   I had just read Natural Cures. I made my official Vegan Proclamation around that time with my incredible friend who helped me a great deal, Sara Carr. Pledging goodbye to cheese (and subsequently allergies) forever! Soon after that I ordered my first Colonix kit. There was absolutely no turning back after that!

   I had taken the Red Pill!

   The things I have learned and the way my life has unfolded after that point is just fascinating. I am so grateful and humbled by the way things work together in our journey through life. I am excited for you all to discover the zest for life that I have been blessed with along my path.

   Ever since then I have felt amazing! You will too!

### Earthlings – Parts I,II,III

OMG!! This is a graphic video. I just saw this a year or two ago. Sit down and be prepared. There are 3 parts, about animal cruelty/abuse, food and farms, then finally animals grown for clothes. It is absolutely life changing! This is the kind of stuff that you don't want to think about. But it is time that we confront the things that we are consuming. We are either going to change, or destroy the earth as well as our bodies. As humans, our lifestyles have to change. Watch this documentary and you will see what I am talking about.

That is your dinner last night bro! Real talk. Wake up and start learning where your food is coming from man. You are what you eat!!

### The Great American The Whole Food Farmacy License to Kill

This is like a more up to date version of the Rave Diet. I highly recommend it. It has details about the hospitals, foods, hidden ingredients, etc. ~ the American food industry and Medical Association is garbage. That is the bottom line.

### Zeitgeist – part I

This isn't about food at all, although it will leave your mouth wide open! (And your eyes.) Zeitgeist is about the sun, history, religion, lies, truth and history. There is a part one and two. For most of you I would recommend you watch the first segment of part 1, which is on religion, and stop the watching there. Watch it again. Take your time. This is truly earth shattering! My jaw was on the floor! You can see it on YouTube I'm sure.

**ra one**
Publications